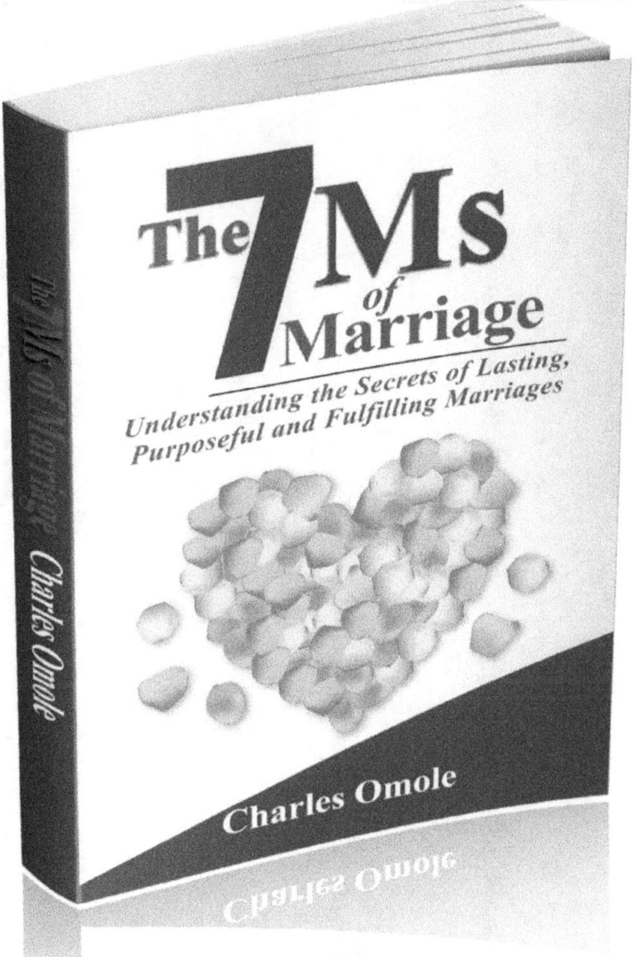

The 7 Ms of Marriage
Understanding the Secrets of Lasting, Purposeful and Fulfilling Marriages
Charles Omole
The 7 Ms of Marriage Charles Omole

ISBN: 978-1907095160

Published by:

London . New York . Lagos

TABLE OF CONTENTS

INTRODUCTION

Marriage is an institution the world system have tried to define and contain within its limited understanding and changing societal worldview. Yet the manufacturer manual (the Bible) has a clear definition and purpose for it.

Sadly many Christians have been caught up in the satanic agenda to redefine marriage and its purpose. To many it is merely a contract. And as we all know, a contract can be changed and even terminated.

But marriage is a covenant according to the word of God. So our attitude and approach must be different if we are to achieve God's intent goal.

I was meditating in scriptures prior to the wedding of a dear spiritual daughter of mine, looking for what the Lord will have me share. That was when the Holy Spirit revealed these seven Ms of marriage. They capture the totality of God's agenda for marriage enjoyment, endurance and longevity.

So congratulations for picking up this book as you will read profound truth you will not find anywhere else. This is probably the most forthright book on marriage you will ever read. If you are divorced, God is a God of new beginning. You can still learn from this book to make your future marriage an unbreakable one. If you are single, then you have a lot of information at your disposal to make the best decision knowing what awaits you. And for those currently married; this book will show you how you can turn thing around, perfect your union and make your marital life a fulfilling one.

Enjoy and be blessed as you read.

Dr Charles Omole
London, 2016.

CHAPTER 1

UNDERSTANING THE ROOT CAUSE OF MARITAL CONFLICT

Volcanoes are common to many countries but one thing scientists have confirmed is that the day a volcano erupts to the surface is not the day the eruption started. It would have started its journey years and weeks earlier but unseen under the surface. Similarly, one of the fundamental phenomenon over the last few years has been the phenomenon called sinkholes. You might have seen it in the media where a huge hole suddenly appear in the middle of nowhere (streets, gardens, highways etc).

It is reasonable to assume that the day the massive hole appear is not that the day the structural problem was created. The weaknesses in the structure of that soil was there for a long time. It is just that one day it became unbearable and simply manifest as the sinkhole that we all see.

Fig. 1 : *An example of a Sinkhole*[1]

The same thesis applies when people have challenges in relationships and marriages. The day you fight is not the day you fought, so to speak. The fundamentals of the fight was there all along. It is just that one day, things simply

[1] <http://www.cnn.com/2013/03/01/us/florida-sinkhole-explainer/> accessed on 15 March 2016

boiled over to a conflict. The right temperature for boiling point was reached.

There are some troubling trends and statistics about marriages that many are only too familiar with; especially in the West. In the United States of America for example, it is claimed that 32% of born-again marriages end in divorce, 52% of churches plunge into major conflict daily in the US, 1500 pastors quit the ministry every month, 34% of pastors are serving congregations that fought with or forced out his predecessor. I am sure many other Western nations could have similar trend with the USA.

In this Chapter, I want us to examine the root cause of conflict in relationships and marriages, before we open the envelope on the seven Ms of marriage. By the end of this chapter, I am sure you will know how to avoid conflict in your marriage and rescue your relationship from the brink of perpetual conflict.

It is so simple that some of you will wonder how come you have not heard of that all along. Truth is, if you don't understand the root cause of conflict, but simply trying to deal with its symptoms, things will not work out well.

So in this chapter, we will be going to the root cause of what causes conflict in marriages and how with the help of God, we can uproot the main causation rather than just dealing with its effects.

If you understand this truth, you will know how to manage your relationship better, since you are now aware of what is at the root cause of the conflict.

There are so many things that causes conflict. Some common problems are:

- innocent misunderstanding
- gossip
- careless words

- unmanaged stress or change
- competition over limited resources
- moral failure
- worldly attitude
- desires unaccomplished

The list can be endless. But beneath these factors is a fundamental cause of conflict that many do not appreciate.

The Bible says: *"And though one can overpower him who is alone, two can resist him. A cord of three strands is not quickly broken."*[2]

The first important thing you need to understand as a Christian is that your marriage is not just about the two of you. You need to appreciate this fundamental truth. It is not just about the two of you. When you take on an appointment as a country's ambassador to a foreign nation; it is no longer just about your personal views any more.

[2] Ecclesiastes 4:12 (AMPLIFIED VERSION)

You will have to represent the views of your elected national leaders in the foreign posting, even if you don't understand or agree with it. Marriage is an office that once occupied; it is no longer about just the two of you. There is now an institutional imperative for you to represent God, the designer and constructor of marriage.

God is also always involved in Christian marriages. Once you invite and commit your marriage to Him, God becomes part of that contract. If your marriage is purely about the two of you, then you are not any different from unbelievers.

There are many reasons people give for why conflict takes place. Some have already been listed but in the remainder of this Chapter, I want us to get to the root of what causes marital conflicts.

To do this properly, we need to go back to the book of Genesis. From the very beginning.

The Bible says in Genesis Chapter three that: *"And when the woman saw that the tree was good for food, and that it was delightful to look at, and a tree to be desired in order to make one wise and insightful, she took some of its fruit and ate it; and she also gave some to her husband with her, and he ate."*[3]

To fully understand the root cause of conflict, I will like to quote this Bible passage from the New Living Translation as this draws attention to a key element of the fall of man in the garden.

*"The woman was **convinced**. She saw that the tree was beautiful and its fruit looked delicious, and she wanted the wisdom it would give her. So she took some of the fruit and ate it. Then she gave some to her husband, who was with her, and he ate it, too."*[4]

The Bible says the woman was CONVINCED. That was before any physical action took place, that is; before she ever eat the fruit

---

[3] Genesis 3:6 (AMPLIFIED VERSION)
[4] Genesis 3:6 (NEW LIVING TRANSLATION)

physically. The deed was done before she physically consumed the fruit. The woman was convinced. Then after the conviction, she ate the fruit.

The moment she was convinced the root cause was created and an invisible chain reaction started that manifested physically in her eating of the fruit. The woman was convinced and at the point of conviction she was committed to eating the fruit.

Eating of the fruit was a consequential inevitability of her conviction. Many have wrongly believed that Eve fell when she eat the fruit, that is not true. She fell at her point of conviction.

The moment she was convinced, the deed was done. Similarly, when there is conflict in a marriage; the root cause of the conflict was initiated long before the actual conflict took place. It is futile to try to solve the conflict by treating its effects, rather than addressing the root cause. So whenever there is conflict in a marriage, there is always ONE main root cause. What is this root cause.

The root cause of marital conflict is DESIRE. The root of all conflict in marriage is desire and we are going to examine how this work and what it means. It may manifest in different grievances and arguments but at its root is an unmet desire.

"Then Abram believed in (affirmed, trusted in, relied on, remained steadfast to) the Lord; and He counted (credited) it to him as righteousness (doing right in regard to God and man)."[5]

In Genesis chapter 15 quoted above, Abraham was credited with righteousness at the point of his believing God, even though he hadn't done anything physically yet. He had not sacrificed Isaac yet, but the Bible says he believed and from that point, he was CREDITED with righteousness.

---

[5] Genesis 15:6 (AMPLIFIED VERSION)

So he was credited at the point of believing, even though practical actions followed latter. Just as Eve eat the fruit at the point of conviction, even though the physical eating followed after.

"Then he said to the woman, "I will sharpen the pain of your pregnancy, and in pain you will give birth. And you will desire to ***control your husband****, but he* ***will rule over you****."*[6]

So from the beginning of the fall of mankind the desire of the woman has been to control her husband. The husband seeing that decided okay, I will rule over you.

Before the fall that was not the case but it became so, the moment man fell for the perverted wisdom of Satan. We have seen the emergence and the beginning of conflict in marriages.

[6] Genesis 3:16 (NEW LIVING TRANSLATION)

"If you do well [believing Me and doing what is acceptable and pleasing to Me], will you not be accepted? And if you do not do well [but ignore My instruction], sin crouches at your door; its desire is for you [to overpower you], but you must master it."[7]

So the genesis of conflict in relationship is desire. That's why the Bible states that:

"Where do wars and fights come from among you? Do they not come from your DESIRES for pleasure that war in your members?"[8]

Do you not see that? Do they not come from this your desires for pleasure that war in your members the bible emphatically stated. War and Fight have their root cause in Desire.

Hence James is saying that conflict is caused at its roots by desire; desire for emotional stuff, for sexual stuff, for physical stuff. It doesn't

---

[7] Genesis 4:7 (AMPLIFIED VERSION)
[8] James 4:1 (NKJV)

matter what it is, the root of marital conflict is desire.

This is the trap the enemy have set for Christians. The enemy has set the trap and many have allowed desire to mess things up big time. First thing you need to understand is that Satan is a person, but Satan is also an office. Allow me to explain.

Satan is a person, but Satan is also an office. This means if you start to do things that are specialists of Satan; you have entered into his office, and he can now easily play and manipulate you.

In the Bible, when Jesus said to Peter *"get you behind me Satan"*,[9] He wasn't saying Peter was Satan. He was saying *what you just express is the thought pattern of Satan* so you can enter the office of Satan by doing things that are his job to do.

---

[9] Matthew 16:23

So you can conduct yourself in such a way that you entered the office of Satan and begin to play out satanic scripts. In life everything starts with a desire, the moment that desire is not met there is trouble. That junction is where conflict begins.

Unmet desires are then escalated and progressed to stage two, DEMAND. You now begin to demand and once your demand is not met, you proceed further to the next stage, JUDGEMENT. And from judgement you proceed to PUNISHMENT.

Fig. 2 : Progression of conflict

Desire, demand, judgement, and punishment; these are the critical stages in conflict development. Now let's start with the first stage conflicts always begin with; desire.

Desire stage

There are wrong desires but some desires are not necessarily wrong. When a legitimate desire has been expressed, but remains unmet by your spouse and show no signs or willingness to change then we have a problem. What you do next will determine if conflict will be birthed or not.

What do you do? You've expressed you desire to your spouse. What do you do if you get a brick wall response? You have two options:

1. You can either remain at the desire level and hand that situation over to God and trust Him for change and a way out, or
2. You can escalate it to the next stage; Demand.

The moment you enter the demand stage, you have entered satanic territory. You have given up on Christ's intervention and entered the zone of Do It Yourself activities.

Remaining in 'desire' while trusting God allows Him to intervene but many simply escalate desire into demand, thus feeding the dynamics of conflict. Once we move from desire into demand then conflict begins.

Demand stage

Demand is the next stage if desire is escalated. At this stage, we have concluded that we must have that thing desired (whatever it is) in order to have a fulfilled life. *"I just have to have that thing, I need it".*

If your spouse does not respond positively to your legitimate desire, if you make that desire a "must have" for your marriage to work, or for you to be happy, you have move from desire to demand. You have crossed the boundary.

At desire you say I wish I can have XY but at demand you say I must have XY. That is now demand stage and once you are in 'demand' you have left grace, you are not into works.

The moment you leave desire and you move to demand, you have activated the chain of conflict. You are in 'demand' when you are now consumed by your unmet desires. It now becomes your all consuming thoughts in the morning when you wake up till you go to bed at night.

That's all you think about so it's all consuming. It's no longer desire you've now moved into demand. At this stage, you have made that desire (even though it is legitimate) a controlling influence over your life.

You have come to see that desire which is now your demand as something you must have. But we must learn how to stay in "Desire" and trust God with our desires rather than escalating them into demand. Because the moments we cross to demand we exclude God from intervening.

The Bible states concerning the Jews:
*"So these nations **feared** the Lord, **yet served their carved images**; also their children and their*

children's children have continued doing as their fathers did, even to this day."[10]

It is a contradiction is it not? The Bible says *"These nations feared the Lord"*. At this point, all sounds good, doesn't it. But the next part of the sentence states that *"Yet serve their carved images"*.

How can they fear God and serve idols at the same time? This is what we do when even though we are saved, we allow escalated desires to create idols in our lives that feed the passion of Satan and moves us out of the realm of grace into works. So we are serving God, but yet holding on to our idols of demand-fortified desires.

Satan is also an office. So whenever you stay in the place where you have become the accuser of another believer, doing what Satan specialises in as the accuser of the brethren[11], you stepped into the office of Satan. The

---

[10] 2Kings 17:41 (NKJV)
[11] Revelations 12:10 (NKJV)

moment you start accusing your brethren you've stepped into his office, you are doing his job for him.

It seems the reason many people always want to escalate desire into demand is because they don't really understand that their marriage is not just about the two of them as Christians.

This ignorance of the presence of Christ in a Christian marriage make many to resort to Do It Yourself (DIY) solution to marital issues which leads into full blown conflict.

Understanding that the presence of Christ (as the third party to a Christian marriage) will enable you to utilise the right escalation process of handing all issues to the Lord because He cares for you,[12] thus keeping you in the 'desire' stage where grace can locate you.

---

[12] 1 Perter 5:7 (NKJV)

Give your 'desires' to the Lord and do not escalate to demand. Doing this will ensure no root of conflict ever develops in your marriage.

So the nations feared the Lord, still served their own idols. Which idol are you holding onto? Which escalated demand, escalated desire are you holding on to that you're ruining your marriage for?

That is the question you should ask yourself as you read this book. Because if you hand the situation over to God and you allow God to process it, you will come through.

Just like Joseph got a visit from God to keep Mary as his wife,[13] you need to understand that God will intervene to minister peace to your home if you hand over your desires to Him, without escalating it to 'demand'. God has a way of making it work, but you must remain at the 'desire stage'.

---

[13] Matthew 1:20 (NKJV)

Judgement stage

When 'demand' does not produce what you want, it will then automatically escalate into 'judgment'. What is 'judgment'? Judgement is when you have now concluded that you spouse will not or cannot change to meet your desires.

Statements like, "My husband never listens", "My wife will never change", these are statements coming out of 'judgment'. You seem to have finalized your spouse. You have marked the script, you have given him/her a score, you have published the result so to speak. "My wife can never do that" is an example statement.

But how do you know she can never do that? Are you God? Judgment stage allows an unmet desire (albeit legitimate) to become a settled root of conflict with no change envisaged.

The moment you begin to say things that seem to confirm and entrench your grievance against your spouse, you move from demand, you are now into judgment.

Your Pastor says, *"why not try x and why to fix your marriage"*, and your quick response is *"Pastor with all due respect, you don't know my wife or you don't know my husband….he/she can never change"*. That is judgment at work.

You have concluded that the other person can never change. You now come to expect that bad behaviour from that person even before the bad behaviour manifests.

You are now a prophet and all the bad things you expect and say happens. This stage allows you to become justified in your anger and thus begin to look for ways to avenge your self and punish your spouse.

The challenge of the 'judgment phase' is that your body language changes. So much so that the response of your spouse will now seem to line up with your perverse expectation, in such a way that you can now say *"Did I not tell you he/she will never change?"*. This becomes case of self fulfilling prophesies.

So once you enter the 'judgment' stage you are lost and you are deep into conflict. I beseech you not to leave the 'desire' level. The further you go up the scale, the more dangerous it is.

Spouse should feel free to express their desires to each other, hoping the other party will receive it and act on it. But if that does not happen simply hand the matter over to Christ and let it go. Do not escalate to demand stage as that will trigger the root of conflict to be created.

Punishment stage

It is very easy to move from demand to judgment and then from judgment to punishment. In satanic realm Satan always demand for sacrifice. Once you work by satanic rules at the 'punishment stage' your spouse will have to pay for the unmet desire.

At the punishment stage somebody has to pay for the unmet desire. This can lead to abuse, separation or even divorce. *"I will show her"* is an example of punishment because you felt a legitimate desire that has not been met.

You've upgraded it from judgment to punishment. Now you feel the other party has to be punished. This is why there is a high rate of divorce in our society.

Punishment stage is when the marriage look irretrievable damaged. Both parties are committed to the path of destruction that is not helping the marriage.

Bitterness and strife have created entrenched positions of anger and disappointment. This is conflict at its worst. Acrimony and divorce is the order of the day at this stage.

I tell people there's little point in divorcing. If you divorce the man or the woman you're going to meet next will have their own problem. You are merely exchanging one misery for another one.

The new man might be good at what your current husband is bad at, but he will certainly also be bad at what your current spouse is good at. So you are merely trading mysteries you are not solving any problem.

What people don't understand about marriage is the fact that God never gives you the complete finished product. What he gives you is the raw material and many people fail to understand their job in marriage is to shape and fine tune one another.

So if you see something you don't like in your spouse, that is something you need to work on fine-tuning over time. This should be a basis for conflict. You've just got to manage the project instead of abandoning your project.

Because we focus on the outcome, we don't look at the process. The process is very essential. It takes total submission to God and casting all our cares on Him to enable Him intervene unhindered in our marriages.

So how do we shape one another. There are spiritual dimensions but there are practical dimensions as well. We will examine these factors in later chapter of the book.

There is no unworkable marriage. It's only that we have different price to pay to make it work. I tell couples even if you marry the wrong person it can work but you have to pay a higher price. It is in the price to pay that many of us falter.

So you need to ask yourself some key question today. Have I moved away from desire to demand? Am I now in judgement or am I in the punishment stage? What are the spirits you have allowed to create stronghold into your life as a result of your escalated demand?

Do the analysis. What happened to the happy you? What happened to the lovely you that existed before? I'm not saying you should gloss over issues but learn to cast your desire unto God.

He can change people faster than you can cause trouble. Desire that is unmet is the heart of conflict in a relationship. Arrested at the desire stage and you will avoid destructive conflict in your home. Cast all your cares on to the Lord. The Bible says through prayer and supplication's make your request known unto God.[14] Don't escalate that desire, be patient while God sort things out on your behalf.

This knowledge means we can save our marriages. The things you are asking and expecting your spouse to provide only God can provide. Real marriage is not a union of two incomplete people, but a union of two complete people.

---

[14] Philippians 4:6 (NKJV)

Adam was sitting quietly and God said it is '*not good for man to be alone*'.[15] This is a profound statement by God. Because how can man be alone, when he was with God.

The Bible says God came in the cool of the day to play with Adam, so how can man be alone? This is a loaded question. However, it is an acknowledgement by God that there are certain needs Adam had that only someone at his level can meet. Praise God. Yet many feel they married the wrong person soon after marriage.

Marriage reveal their true character and weaknesses unseen before marriage. If you've never thought you married the wrong person, you've not been married long enough.

But you have develop the habit of doing the right things regardless of your feelings. A lady went to a divorce lawyer seeking a divorce from her husband. She told the lawyer she

---

[15] Genesis 2:18 (NKJV)

want the most painful divorce ever because she has been hurt for a long time. So the lawyer said *"okay, I need about 28 days to prepare the paperwork"*.

The lawyer then stated that to make this the most painful one for the husband, there is something she must do. From tonight, advised the lawyer, when you go home, give him the best sex ever, prepare his best meal and say everything you know he likes it hear.

The woman said *why would I say that, I want to divorce him and not stroke his ego*? But the lawyer said you know when you say all those things he will relax and starts thinking you are back in love with him. So in 30 days you just give him the divorce paper and that will be a most painful act.

The woman agreed that this approach will be a clever move. So she went home and started all she was advised. She gave him the best sex of his life, prepared his best meal. After two weeks she called the lawyer she said I don't want to divorce again. The lawyer asked what happened? She said her husband has changed. She said *"I didn't know my husband is this sweet."* What happened?

As she changed her behaviour (albeit acting a script), her husband responded by changing his response to her, but his was for real. Hence, action more readily come before feeling. It is easier to act your way into a feeling than to feel your way into an action.

In this case, you see she was doing those things even though she didn't feel it but by law of life there is a corresponding reaction that must be created. If she was told to do that to save her marriage se would not have done it. But the husband seeing the 'new' her also responded.

Within two weeks of acting out some actions, the feelings came back. So we can save our relationships if we understand that our feeling is not the basis for a decision.

For those reading this that have ongoing unresolved conflict in your marriage, ask yourself which stage you are. Ask yourself which stage you are? Are you in demand stage? Are you in judgement or in punishment? Retrace your step back and commit your issue(s) over to God. Stay at the desire level and allow God to do what only he can do.

Scriptural Counsel

There is an important scriptural reminder of the need for both partners to stay in the desire zone and not escalate their unmet desires.

Take the story of Sarah, Abraham's wife. Her husband asked her to lie that she was his sister when they entered a new land, especially as the king showed interest in her.[16] Knowing this lie could open her to being rapped and abused by men who think she is single, Sarah complied with her husbands request. What

[16] Genesis 20 (NKJV)

will make a wife to obey her husband even at the risk of personal arm to herself?

The answer to this question reveals the pivotal role God plays in a Christian marriage. He is always on hand to intervene if given the chance by remaining in the desire zone and in prayer.

In 1Peter Chapter 3, verses 1-2, wives are encouraged to obey their husbands, even if it appears the husband is not obeying the word of God.

"Wives, obey your own husbands. Some of your husbands may not obey the Word of God. By obeying your husbands, they may become Christians by the life you live without you saying anything."[17]

That is a tough ask in a world of radical feminism that wives should obey their husbands regardless. But if you want God to

[17] 1 Perter 3:1 (New Life Version)

intervene in your marriage you must not cross the desire line.

There is a need for both parties to develop a strong personal relationship with God as couples. It is your confidence in God that will see you protected and vindicated after obeying your husband in circumstances you may not agree with.

Mary submitted herself to God and accepted whatever Joseph was going to do to her, due to her 'unexplained' pregnancy. But God intervened by dealing with Joseph who then took her as his wife.

In the case of Sarah, she obeyed seemingly difficult instructions from her husband, but had no fear due to her personal trust in God, who again vindicated and protected her. Couples need to understand that they are not alone in their marriage,. God is there and His powers are limitless on our behalf.

It is true that in the particular case of Abraham referenced before, his safety was partly a consideration in Sarah's mind. But that is not all she considered. In Sarah's lifestyle as a wife, it is revealed what happened and why she obeyed the instructions of her husband.

"This was the kind of beauty seen in the holy women who lived many years ago. They put ***their hope in God****. They also* ***obeyed*** *their husbands."*[18]

"This is how the holy women of old made themselves beautiful. They put their ***trust in God*** *and* ***accepted the authority of their husbands****."*[19]

"For this is the way the holy women, who ***put their hope in God****, used to beautify themselves long ago –* ***being submitted to their own husbands****"*[20]

---

[18] 1 Peter 3:5 (New Life Version)
[19] 1 Peter 3:5 (New Living Translation)
[20] 1 Peter 3:5 (Tree of Life Version)

As can be seen from the scripture, Sarah Trusted God fully not her husband. She trusted God and that trust made it possible to obey her husband's instruction. Our total trust MUST be in God and not just in each other. Both parties are fallible in marriage and it takes God to hold the two together. God cannot disappoint hence, He is absolutely trustworthy.

Sarah trusted God and was assured of His protection and care. Without full personal trust in God, obedience will be impossible in marriage.

Also, without a trust in God, husbands cannot truly love their wives. They will simply be limited to knowing them by the flesh, rather than by the spirit.

Trusting God, allows the husband to love his wife regardless of what he sees physically to the contrary. Knowing that God is able to turn her around to the wife he desires. Things can only work in marriage when both parties rely on God and trust Him personally. That way, feelings towards each other is slightly irrelevant. You stay because you trust God.

I have heard wives say to me, *"I don't trust my husband"*. Well…that may not be the big problem you think it is. Trust God and allow Him to deal with your husband in ways you cannot personally. True infallible trust cannot be invested in a human being, they will fail you.

- Wives; trust God and obey your husbands, regardless of the foolishness of the instruction. Allow your trust in God to assure you of protection and vindication.
- Husbands, trust God and love your wives regardless of what you see in them to the contrary. Allow the trust in God to compel your unconditional love.

Of course there is a common sense limit to obeying your husbands risky instructions. If Abraham had asked Sarah to go and murder somebody; she would have rightly refused. That will be a clear breach of boundary. But in this case, Abraham and Sarah were actually blood relations in reality.

So his assertion is not a full lie but just an incomplete declaration. Therefore, this command relates to instructions about the direction, composition and operation of the home, where to live, which church to attend and general household matters.

This is not about obeying illegal instructions. This caveat is important so as not to use this as an excuse to oppress one another.

Also all disagreements in couples I have seen are not about illegal instructions in the home. Its about basic stuff like, which school the children will attend, who they are allowed to associate with, disobedience to instruction not to spend or travel and so on. These are the sort of instructions the bible expects the wives to obey while trusting God for a good outcome.

As a father of four daughters, and a Lawyer and Judge, I will not promote illegality in the name of marital obedience.

So let it be clear, this obedience espoused by scripture has to do with normal household decision making and not a breach of the law of the land. Why? Because the bible instructs to obey lawful authorities. Hence, the bible cannot contradict itself.

"Therefore submit yourselves to every ordinance of man for the Lord's sake, whether to the king as supreme, or to governors, as to those who are sent by him for the punishment of evildoers and for the praise of those who do good. For this is the will of God, that by doing good you may put to silence the ignorance of foolish men – as free, yet not using liberty as a cloak for vice, but as bondservants of God. Honour all people. Love the brotherhood. Fear God. Honour the king."[21]

---

[21] 1 Peter 2:13-17 (NKJV)

So as you can see, illegality cannot be supported by scripture in the name of obedience to husband. But the key point is that both parties have to put their trust in God and they will be able to fulfil their part of the bargain based on that foundation.

Prayer

Lord, I pray that you grant everyone reading this book the wisdom to be able to remain at the desire level. Thus avoiding themselves being used as tools by the enemy. We thank you for the testimony that this book will produce, we thank you for the turnaround in relationships that we will see as a result. We thank you Father for the joy of marriage that will be rekindled as your people read this book. We pray that concerning all the couples that will read this book, I declare that the best is yet to come in Jesus' name we pray.

Hallelujah!

CHAPTER 2

ESSENTIAL KEYS FOR A CONFLICT-FREE MARRAIGE

We are all born male or female, to be a man or a woman is by choice. Being a man is an office. Many assume that because you have a beard or you are a certain age, you have male genitals then these make you a man. In fact in our society today it doesn't make you a man at all anyway, you know.

But the point I'm trying to make is being a man is an office you occupy only in reference to your relationship with God. It is your relationship with God that defines your manhood.

A male that has no good relationship with God remains a male. So a male occupies three offices:

- The male occupies the office of the man in terms of his relationship with God.
- He occupies the office of the husband in terms of a relationship with the wife and
- Occupies the office of the father in front of the relationship with the children.

Likewise, the female occupies three offices in the office of a woman in terms of our relationship with God.

The office of a wife in terms of her relationship with her husband and the office of a mother in terms of the relationship with the children.

Now there is a primary purpose rule in the kingdom which is if something fails in its primary purpose it will definitely feel in any secondary application.

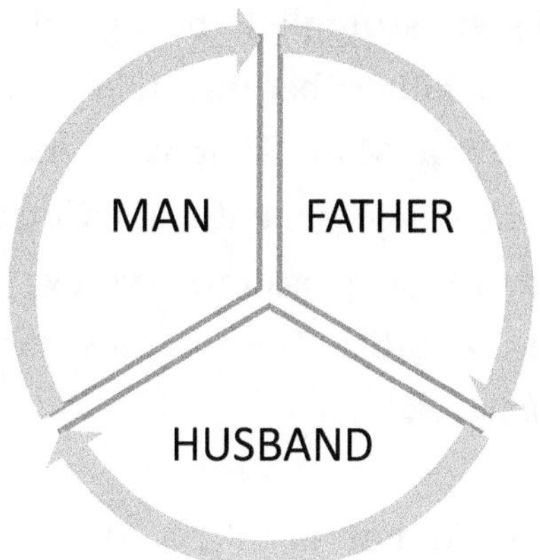

FIG. 3 : *Three Dimensional offices of a Male*

Similarly a female also occupy three offices as illustrated below.

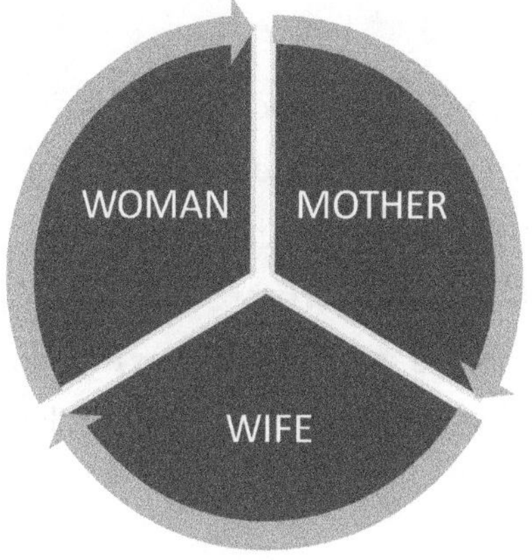

FIG. 4 : Three Dimensional offices of a Female

So a male will struggle to be a good husband and a good father; because these are offices reserved for a Man. That is every time in scripture marriage is mentioned, God uses the word 'man'. He assumes you've already occupied that office, "*for this cause shall a man leave his father...*".

The bible did not say "...a Male leave his father.." So God already assumes manhood but the challenge we have in our world today is that a lot of males are getting married and when the male gets married to the female then must have problems.

They tend to occupy secondary offices when they've not occupied the primary one. So it's important that you understand all things start with God. It's important that you lay that foundation of a relationship with God. You must be a man by virtue of your relationship with God.

At this point, let me explain a basic concept I will be using in this book. A lot of the principles apply to both man and woman. So if I use a 'he', be sure it applies to a 'she' as well. I am trying to avoid using a he/she all the time. So if I note something from a male perspective it means exactly the same thing from a female perspective could apply.

Getting married is not compulsory. It is not a requirement to make heaven. So you don't have to. But once you decide to do so, then you have to play by the rules set by the designer of the institution.

In a book I wrote a few years back[22], I explained the need for foundation of love to exist for Christian marriages. I will like to quote elements of its content at this point.

The Foundation of Love in a Christian Marriage.

"For God so loved the world that he gave his one and only Son, that whoever believes in him shall

[22] Charles Omole, *Journey into Fulfilment*

not perish but have eternal life."[23]

"Love is patient, love is kind. It does not envy, it does not boast, it is not proud. 5 It is not rude, it is not self-seeking, it is not easily angered, it keeps no record of wrongs. 6 Love does not delight in evil but rejoices with the truth. 7 It always protects, always trusts, always hopes, always perseveres. Love never fails. But where there are prophecies, they will cease; where there are tongues, they will be stilled; where there is knowledge, it will pass away. 9 For we know in part and we prophesy in part, 10 but when perfection comes, the imperfect disappears. 11 When I was a child, I talked like a child, I thought like a child, I reasoned like a child. When I became a man, I put childish ways behind me."[24]

Love is a decision- carefully and sensibly made.

- It is not blind.
- You don't fall into it.
- You don't fall out of it.

---

[23] John 3:16 (NKJV)

[24] 1 Cor. 13:4-11 (NKJV)

Love is a commitment to stay in love with the one you are committing to. Because of love's divine quality, it can do just that. It's capacity transcends the imperfections of your spouse and your limitations as a man / woman.

Love is an act of the will. You deliberately choose to live it. The feelings add to the depth and fulfilment of love; but they do not in themselves indicate the presence of true love.

Dr. Robert Sternberg, a University psychologist, pioneered and developed a scientific model of love.

In his model, love like a triangle, has three sides. Each side represents the three essential ingredients for conjugal love- within the marriage setting. They are:

PASSION INTIMACY
COMMITMENT

ROMANTIC LOVE

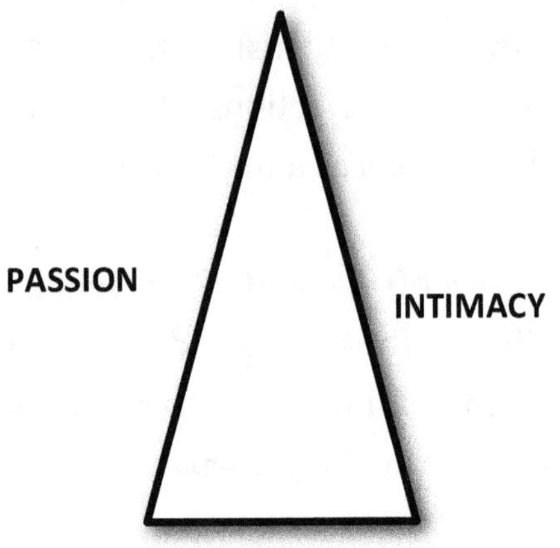

Key Characteristics of Romantic Love:

- ✓ Passion & attraction are the basis for love
- ✓ But they fluctuate with feelings & hormones
- ✓ Low commitment leads to unfaithfulness

Result : Unstable, unhealthy, immature & unchristian

FOOLISH LOVE

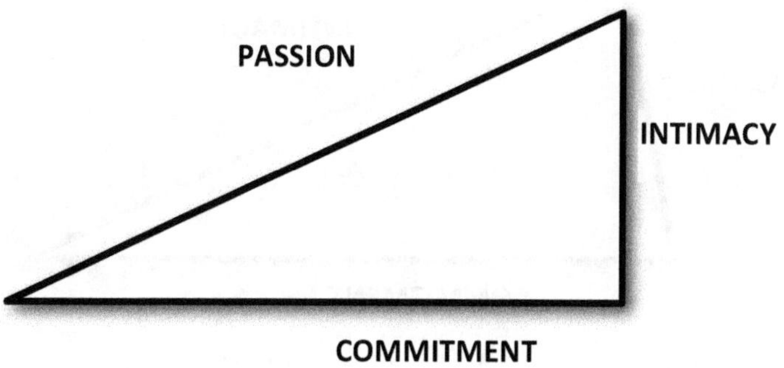

Key Characteristics of Foolish Love:

- ✓ Passion is the basis for commitment
- ✓ Therefore, a reduction in passion produces insecurity and distant feelings
- ✓ The low level of intimacy produces feelings of bitterness

Result: Committed as long as sex (passion) is good, unfaithfulness.

FRIENDSHIP LOVE

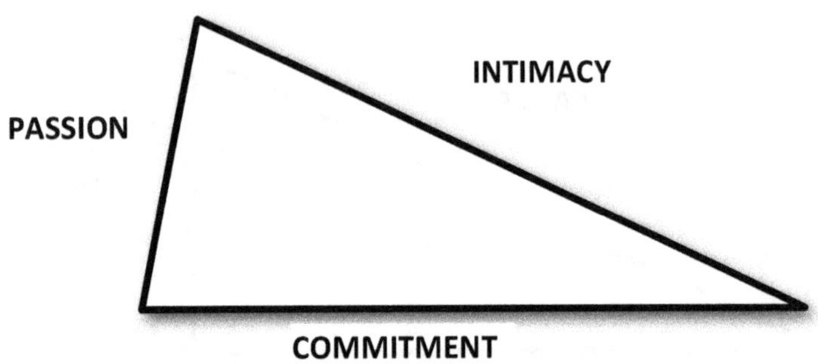

Key Characteristics of Friendship Love:

- ✓ Passion fades (Aging, excessive busyness, sexual failures)
- ✓ Love based on security of the friendship (Intimacy) & commitment developed over a long time.

Result: Will stay together as good friends, but have an unfulfilled Passion, Romantic & sex life.

CONSUMMATE LOVE

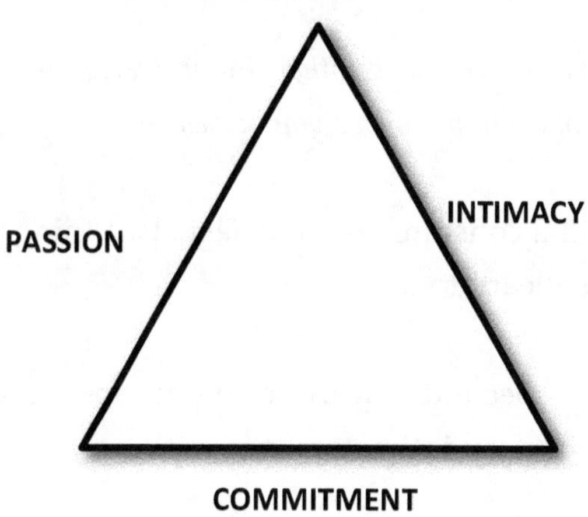

Key Characteristics of Consummate Love:

- ✓ To balance all three components should be the goal of every couple.
- ✓ The Body needs & feeds on Passion
- ✓ The Soul needs & feeds on Intimacy
- ✓ The Spirit needs Commitment.

Learning to Recognise Your Spouse's Needs

"Be devoted to one another in brotherly love. Honour one another above yourselves."[25]

To build a consummate marriage, two things you must learn to do are:

- Become aware of your spouse's deep intimate needs.
- Develop the capacity to meet them lovingly.

When two people commit to each other, and agree to 'forsake all others' for life, they have high expectations.

While some of these expectations may be unreasonable and overbearing, the intense and intimate needs are not. The few basic needs that are reserved to be met within the

---

[25] Rom. 12: 10 (NKJV)

marriage setting form the basis of the LOVE BANK PRINCIPLE.

Dr. William F. Harley's Findings[26]

As a general rule, I do not believe in Christian living their lives according to some scientific research or findings. We are all too unique for such findings to be accurate in light of divine truth. But I am convinced that these findings reflect the situation of many men and women across the world to include in this book.

This by no means describes every man or woman on this planet, so you may be an exception. But many people will ultimately find it useful.

After interviewing hundreds of couple, Dr. William F. Harley came up with three main conclusions.[27]

Three conclusions reached:

---

[26] William Harley, *His Needs Her Needs,* Revel Publishers 2001
[27] William Harley, *His Needs Her Needs,* Revel Publishers 2001

- ✓ Men and women have different basic needs.
- ✓ Men and women expect different things from a relationship.
- ✓ Understanding those needs and developing the capacity to meet them is a crucial key to a joyful home.

THE LOVE BANK PRINCIPLE[28]

"Let us therefore follow after the things which make for peace, and things wherewith one may edify another."[29]

1. Each of us has a Love Bank.

Your Love Bank contains one account for each person you know. People either make deposits or withdrawals when we interact with them.

Pleasurable experiences make a deposit and produce happiness. Painful and unpleasant ones make a withdrawal and produce a feeling

---

[28] William Harley, *His Needs Her Needs,* Revel Publishers 2001

[29] Romans 14: 19 (NKJV)

of loss. Therefore, we naturally gravitate towards investors.

2. The account in your Love Bank fluctuates. Some people have a healthy balance. Others don't change much / or are in the red.

3. Most couples start out with a healthy balance - but then cut down on their investment. Why?

- ✓ Because we do not understand the implications.
- ✓ Because we start to take each other for granted.
- ✓ Because we start to keep an account of the wrongs done to us.

4. **Your goal in marriage is to be the major investor in your spouse's Love Bank.**

- ✓ By finding out what makes your spouse happy.
- ✓ By endeavouring to meet those intimate needs daily....

5. **When this is not done, selfishness and self-centred living is empowered to reign in your home.**

Conclusion

Apart from your Christian walk, your marriage and family life is the most important and crucial commitment you need to make in life.

Your marriage is the training ground God uses in many situations to refine, mature and help you achieve your purpose and destiny here on earth. No wonder the enemy is attacking marriages and homes with all the ammunition he's got.

However, you do not need to be a victim of the enemy's plots. Your Heavenly Father (who instituted marriage), has provided all you need to be victorious in your marriage. It is He alone who can help you to have the marriage

of your dreams. Would you humbly call on Him?
So an essential key to a conflict free marriage is understanding the need to be a Man and Woman before marriage takes place.

And that this happens visa your relationship with God. The other key is to understand the need of each other and work at meeting them.

Remember that: YOU CAN DO ALL THINGS THROUGH CHRIST WHO STRENGTHENS YOU.[30]

[30] Philippians 4:13 (NKJV)

CHAPTER 3

WHAT'S LOVE GOT TO DO WITH IT?

Love in English language has many nuanced variations in Greek (the language in which the New Testament was written). The translators of the Bible use the word "love" to capture multiple words in Greek.

In the Bible, the main Greek words are:

- ✓ Eros
- ✓ Phileo (or sometime used as "Storge")
- ✓ Agape

Eros represents Romantic love, which is what couples tend to have for each other. Phileo represents the emotional bond between say mother and daughter; while Agape is God's kind of love that we are mandated to have towards all people.

Agape is unconditional love. In fact the Bible commands us to love (Agape) our enemies.[31] That is how unconditional it is. Agape says "I love you" period.

But God demonstrates His own love toward us, in that while we were still sinners, Christ died for us.[32]

The reason God's love for you will never change is because His love is not conditional on what you do or do not do. God loves you, full stop. No ifs or buts. This unconditional nature of God's love is what keeps the love consistent and unchanging, despite our many sins and disobedience.

The number one reason men say they married their wives (and vice versa) is Love. This however is usually Eros. But should that be the

---

[31] Matthew 5:43-48 (NKJV)

[32] Romans 5:8 (NKJV)

case? And is that kind of love able to sustain a marriage? Conditional love of any kind cannot sustain a marriage. Especially when weaknesses, betrayals and human faults become apparent.

Eros is a conditional love that says I love you because you love me too. Eros says I love you because you make me happy. You meet my needs.

I love you because of the way you make me feel. All these are ok, but there is a problem. These sentiments are conditional on the state of your emotion. And this fluctuates based on so many factors.

If we are commanded to love our enemies (who do nothing for us); surely loving our spouse should not be too difficult if we put on the Agape garment so to speak. The difficulty is that most people marry for Eros and not Agape.

Eros is not a viable foundation for Christian Marriage. Romantic Love is a bad foundation for marriage. That love does not keep marriage together.

Any divorced person will tell you that something came up that was more powerful that the love (Eros) they claimed to have for each other. It may be infidelity, abuse, addictions etc. But something came that Eros could no longer sustain.

I love Aircrafts…but I cannot fly them. The problem with Eros is that many who claim they have it also lack the knowledge to function in that which they love.

The foundation of all marriages should be Agape, before Eros is developed. This way, when Eros fails, Agape never fail. Too often Christians do not work in Agape as Bible instructed. They simply develop Eros for someone and make that the basis of marriage. It takes unconditional love to build a marriage that stands the test of time.

My people are destroyed for lack of knowledge..... Because you have rejected knowledge, I also will reject you from being priest for Me; Because you have forgotten the law of your God, I also will forget your children. The more they increased, The more they sinned against Me; I will change their glory into shame.[33]

You have rejected knowledge the Bible says. So it is available, but you have refused to learn it. Hence, you cannot be my representative says the Lord. Priest is a representative. Applying it to this topic means that God is saying you cannot represent me in marriage if you are stupid or ignorant of my principles for that institution.

Because you have forgotten the law of your God, I also will forget your children. "The more they increased, The more they sinned against Me; I will change[a] their glory into shame

[33] Hosea 4:6-7-- 6

God says I will forget your children. That means Ignorance can become trans-generational. If you mess up your marriage due to IGNORANCE, there is a good chance your children will do the same.

- ✓ So acquire knowledge for the sake of your children.
- ✓ Read a book for the sake of your children.
- ✓ Attend a seminar for the sake of your children.
- ✓ Work on your marriage for the sake of your children.

Because the more you learn the more you can transfer to them. So you can love someone and still mess them up and mess up your lives in marriage if you lack knowledge to function in that which you love. True love is therefore not an emotion, but a choice and an act of your will.

PROOF: JESUS commanded that we LOVE OUR ENEMIES. That can only happen by choice. Emotion is not required.

Matthew 5:43-48 - *"You have heard that it was said, 'You shall love your neighbour and hate your enemy.' But I say to you, love your enemies, bless those who curse you, do good to those who hate you, and pray for those who spitefully use you and persecute you, that you may be sons of your Father in heaven".*[34]

In marriage, you must love by choice, not emotion. Agape is an essential foundation upon which Eros can be built. That way if Eros fails, Agape will never fail.

"Husbands, love your wives, just as Christ also loved the church and gave Himself for her".[35]

"Husbands, love your wives".[36]

So if Husbands are commanded to love their wives…it means only husbands are truly able to love their wives as God intended.

---

[34] Matthew 5:43-48 (NKJV)
[35] Ephesians 5:25 – 25 (NKJV)
[36] Colossians 3:19 (NKJV)

"On the third day a wedding took place at Cana in Galilee. Jesus' mother was there, and Jesus and his disciples had also been invited to the wedding. When the wine was gone, Jesus' mother said to him, "They have no more wine." "Dear woman, why do you involve me?" Jesus replied. "My time has not yet come." His mother said to the servants, "Do whatever he tells you." Nearby stood six stone water jars, the kind used by the Jews for ceremonial washing, each holding from twenty to thirty gallons. Jesus said to the servants, "Fill the jars with water"; so they filled them to the brim. Then he told them, "Now draw some out and take it to the master of the banquet."

They did so, and the master of the banquet tasted the water that had been turned into wine. He did not realise where it had come from, though the servants who had drawn the water knew. Then he called the bridegroom aside and said, "Everyone brings out the choice wine first and then the cheaper wine after the guests have had too much to drink; but you have saved the best till now. "This, the first of his miraculous signs, Jesus performed at Cana in Galilee. He thus revealed his glory, and his disciples put their faith in him. After this he went down to Capernaum with his mother and brothers and his disciples. There they stayed for a few days".[37]

In these verses we read about the turning of water into wine by Jesus Christ. There are vital lessons we can learn from this story.

PRE-WEDDING LOVE IS DIFFERENT FROM POST-WEDDING LOVE.

If the old wine represents pre-wedding love, then post-wedding love is the new wine. As clearly shown in this story, the initial wine runs out soon after the wedding. This love (Eros) is based largely on infatuation, emotional connection and feelings. it lacks deep and objective knowledge of each other without which you cannot truly love your spouse long-term.

Many married couples notice that a few months into marriage, after the initial

[37] John 2 :1-12 (NKJV)

euphoria and excitement of the wedding wears out, they begin to see a different side of their partner. It's like being brought back to earth after a spell in space.

Now there is nothing wrong with this; as it marks the beginning of the development of the new wine. A new kind of love that says "I know all your weaknesses and bad habits but I still love you". That can only be Agape. A love like this is the one that endures. This is the new wine.

So, the old wine will run out of your marriage at one point or another. Whether you are a believer or not. The difference is that believers have access to the source of the new wine, our Lord Jesus Christ. It needs to run out to enable the new wine, the new refreshing love to evolve. And as it was in the case in Cana, the new wine will be fantastically better than the old wine. That is why you can look your spouse in the eyes twenty years into marriage and say, "I love you more today than I did before we married".

Despite all you've been through together, your love is stronger. But you also know that this new love is way different from the initial love you had before your wedding.

What I am saying is that Agape has to be the real foundation of all marriages, Eros can then be built on it. Eros without Agape foundation will run out soon after marriage.

Successful marriage hinges on the application of knowledge; (Knowing and understanding God's principles). You need to know and understand what it is to be a MAN or a WOMAN

We are all born male and female, to be a man is by Choice. A Male occupies three offices, that is; MAN, HUSBAND and FATHER. Similarly, a Female occupies THREE offices; WOMAN, WIFE and MOTHER. Only MAN and WOMAN can make a success of MARRIAGE not Male and Female.

The Number one reason you should marry is to marry someone that can help you fulfil purpose and destiny that KNOWLEDGE has produced. There has to be destiny/vision alignment and compatibility as much as you know it.

True love (Agape) only evolves with knowledge. And true knowledge of each other only begins after marriage. Agape knows all your mess and craziness and yet still loves you….That is the Foundation needed in marriage. ONLY when Eros and Phileo is built on AGAPE; That PERMANENT RELATIONSHIP is POSSIBLE. But AGAPE is not possible without Knowledge of God's principles.

CHAPTER 4

MERGING THE SPOUSE OF YOUR DREAM AND THE SPOUSE OF YOUR REALITY

We all have dreams of what our spouse will look like. What they will do and what we will do with them. Imaginations are full of things you dream of doing together.

But what happens when the spouse of your dream differ from the spouse of your waking moments. What happens when you feel you have married the wrong person?

Now Laban had two daughters. The older daughter was named Leah, and the younger one was Rachel. There was no sparkle in Leah's eyes, but Rachel had a beautiful figure and a lovely face. Since ***Jacob***

***was in love with Rachel**, he told her father, "I'll work for you for seven years if you'll give me Rachel, your younger daughter, as my wife."*[38]

Jacob was in love with Rachel and worked seven years for her as agreed with her father. For those years he must have imagined daily what their lives together as a couple will be. He must have fantasised in many areas of their relationship. How they will live as a couple, how many children they will have and so on. **Rachel was the wife of his dream.**

"So it came to pass in the morning, that behold, it was Leah…"[39]

Jacob woke up on day one of his marital life to discover that the wife of his dream is different from the wife of his reality. Behold it was Leah not Rachel.

This is exactly what happen in many marriages. Many people have imagined

---

[38] Genesis 29:16-18 (New Living Translation)
[39] Genesis 29:25 (KJV)

'Rachel' all their life only to find that Leah is who they have married.

What do you do when the wife of your dream does not match the wife of your waking moment? You have to work to make both of them one.

One is the wife of your imagination and the other is wife of your reality. Rachel was the first person in Laban's family that Jacob saw while on his way to Laban.

And the Bible says he fell in love with her instantly. He had his own imagination what kind of wife he wanted and what he dreamt doing with her.

So he had everything practically sorted, in his mind. But then what happened. The Bible says Laban swapped the girls. Behold the wife he was seeing after the the wedding was not the wife he imagined. Many will relate with this story in their marriages.

The spouse you now live with is not the spouse you imagined they will be during courtship. What has changed? And how do you unite the two of them, how do you make them one?

This case of Jacob, is instructive on how some people can be caught up with imaginary wife or husband that actually do not correlate with the real one that is in front of them. And for you to have success in marriage you need to learn to make them one. That is to make the wife of your imagination and the wife of your reality to merge into one. As long as you seek 'Rachel' in your dream, but have 'Leah' in reality there will be crisis in that marriage.

You have dreams and fantasies about who you will marry for years. You had your list of attributes and features you wanted in your spouse and you believed you have met your life mate that is your 'Rachel'.

You could not just wait until you marry each other but then after marriage he or she suddenly seemed to be a different person from what you had imagined; you are now facing your Leah. What do you do?

What do you do when your dream conflicts with your reality? To be successful in marriage you need to develop the skills and the ability to make them one. To merge expectation with your reality to create your dream out of the reality.

Strategies to make them One

Success come in marriage when you are able to create your dream from the reality you have in your hands. You may have a dream of an athletic wife for instance; but your actual wife is not into physical exercises.

So your job is to transform the wife of your reality into the wife of your dream. But there is a problem. How do you know if your dream as you understand it is God's settled will for you?

What happens if you have spent time encouraging your spouse to change and transform to be the wife of a dream that then changes? These are some of the elements that lead to crisis in marriage. So what do you need to understand if you are to successfully combine dream and reality? What are the dangers and pitfalls to avoid? What are the essential keys to success?

The wife of your dream is usually based on your own idea of marriage not God's idea. That's the first thing you need to understand. It is your own idea of marriage that created that expectation not God's idea. Because if it's God's idea it will be a different story, but I'll come to this in a moment.

The second thing you need to understand about the wife of your dreams is she is based on your perception or understanding of your dream at a point in time it is not your reflection of the dream God has given you.

Let me give you an example to make it clear. I don't know about you, when I met my wife if somebody told me that I would pastor a church, much less now oversee several churches; I would have said you were kidding. In fact she would have run away immediately.

It was the last thing on either of our agenda. So the wife I had at that time was the wife of a businessman. But as my dream changed, the wife of my dream changed too. My expectations of her changed too.

So I had to work to make the wife of my reality and the wife of my dream same person. Otherwise, there will always be dissatisfaction that your wife (or husband) is not meeting up to the pictures in your imagination of her/him. Such division between dream and reality creates crisis in marriages; when both parties become dissatisfied with each other.

Let me give you another example to make things clearer. You are a rock artist and you are thinking of getting married. And you concluded you need the wife of a rock artist. Wanted somebody who is loud, somebody who is flamboyant, because it goes with your understanding of your dream at that point in time. Years later you became saved.

Few years after, God call you into ministry as a pastor, now you have a problem. Because your wife still dresses like a rock star babe as you insisted. Now you are a pastor and you want her to dress less flamboyantly. But her flamboyance was what you wanted, based on your initial understanding of your dream. That was what you created. The problem with the wife of your dream is that it was based on your understanding of your dream at a point in time. It is not based on the vision God has given you. Now that your reality has changed, how easy do you think your spouse will find it to change?

You cannot truly have a wife of your dream, until your dream is settled and God-given. Until you obtained a certainty of your calling, any spouse of your imagination is self serving and not God driven. So until your dream is settled and clear, you cannot begin to make them one.

It is important that you realise that when you dream of the kind of person to marry, you are basing that on your own unfinished understanding of where you think you are heading? But you don't if upon maturity, God could be sending you in a complete opposite direction.

The other principle you need to understand is this. Before the wife of your dreams can emerge it's a necessity that you must accept the wife of your waking moment. You must accept the wife of your reality first. If Jacob didn't accept Leah, Rachel wouldn't have manifested. You have to accept Leah first then Rachel will come.

You have to accept the wife or husband of your reality. You must accept that reality first then you can begin to work on making them one. Absolutely important. Once you accept the wife of your reality and you obey God's command the wife of your dream will begin to emerge and become a reality.

Jacob worked seven years and then got Leah after the seven years. When he discovered the fraud Laban had perpetrated against him, he was not happy at all.

So Laban said (after agreeing to another seven years labour for Rachel) as is the tradition, *fulfil her days and then you can have Rachel.* And by tradition that mean Jacob had to stay with the first wife (Leah) for 7 days.

Jacob got Rachel seven days later and then worked seven years for her. Did you notice what happened here? Jacob worked seven years and got Leah after, he got Rachel 7 days after that and then works seven years to pay for her bride price.

So he got Leah after labour, he got Rachel before labour. Are you seeing this. He did the seven years and got Leah, he got Rachel and then did seven years after he got her.

Many people think he got Rachel after fourteen years. No. He got Leah after seven years, then got Rachel immediately (after seven days), and then work the seven years after. That is significant. Because the wife of your waking moment (Leah) is real hard work.

The wife of your imagination (Rachel) seems to give you instant gratification because imagination is cheap.

You can sit down in your bedroom and imagine anything you like. Is that not so? You can sit down and imagine anything you like but the wife of your reality is your real work.

It's important for you to see that God only uses the wife of your waking moment to birth destiny and purpose not the wife of your imagination. God will always use the wife of your reality. I wish my wife is X, I wish my wife is Y does not matter. You can wish all you like.

The wife God will use is the one that standing in front of you not the one that is in your head. The transformation of your wife or husband of your reality to the wife of your dreams only truly begins as you mature and your dream is settled. Your dream has to be God led.

It is important that you realise the whole essence of marriage is working to make sure that you are perfecting each other to actualised your dreams from the reality that you are confronted with.

You want lemonade and you have been given lemon. So go to work and use the raw material you have been given to produce the lemonade of your dream.

Now the only way the spouse of your dreams will emerge is if both of you work on making that dream a reality. I hear couples say all the time stuff like:

- ✓ *"She is not the woman I imagined she will be".*
- ✓ *"She is not the way I had imagined my wife would be".*
- ✓ *"I had fantasised how my husband will be but he does not fit that picture".*

The questions are endless. But the common factor is the divergence between the imagined spouse and the real spouse. Many like the imagined one but dislike the real partner.

What we have discussed in this chapter is that you must begin with your "real" spouse on your way to actualising your dream or imagined partner. But you must leave room for change as your ambition and understanding of your dream is progressive. Hence you need a spouse that can adapt with you as you adapt and realign your vision to what God wants it to be.

Do not reject your 'Leah' in your search for 'Rachel'. That will be a mistake. The wife of your waking moment (Leah) will end up birthing the son from whom the Messiah will come, not your Rachel.

Your spouse is the best raw material God has given you to become the spouse of your dream. Do not take each other for granted. Be ready to change and adapt to make your marriage thrive.

Work on each other. Transform one another. Be ready to compromise and make each other happy. You have only one life to live, make it count and stop living in an imaginary world, when you have the real article beside you.

Your spouse today is the raw material. Use that to create your dream world and stop thinking someone else will create that dream arena with you.

CHAPTER SUMMARY

7 LESSONS & FACTS FROM JACOB ON HOW TO MAKE THE SPOUSE OF YOUR DREAM AND THAT OF YOUR REALITY ONE.

1. **WIFE (HUSBAND) OF YOUR DREAM IS USUALLY BASED ON YOUR OWN IDEA OF MARRIAGE.**

a) Wife of your dream is usually based on Your dream not God's dream for you.

b) Your dream can change as you mature in God and discover purpose.

   a. So Wife of your dream is only a snapshot in time based on what you know. The wife of your waking moment is the real deal.

   b. Do you want a wife that is carved (and fixed) in the image of a snapshot of your vision at a fixed moment; or a wife that can suit any situation you find yourself in the future.

        c. So singles should stop looking for a perfect partner....they don't exist.

c) Wife of your dream is usually based on an exaggerated impression and assessment of your own capabilities and attractiveness.
    a. That is; the wife of your dream is usually based on your DREAM image of yourself. (Dream YOU v Dream WIFE)

d) Even dreams that you are certain is given by God can change; much less of your own self-induced dreams.
    a. Example: God told Abraham to Kill Isaac. - God's given dream No.1.
    b. But same God told Abraham to STOP and not Kill Isaac, just as he was obeying. Dream number 2
        i. So which of the two is correct? 1 or 2?
        ii. BOTH ARE CORRECT. God is Sovereign and

cannot be put in a box. So you need a wife (husband) for ALL seasons and not just for one.

2. **YOU MUST FIRST ACCEPT THE WIFE OF YOUR WAKING MOMENT (REALITY) BEFORE THE WIFE OF YOUR DREAMS COULD BE SET LOSE.**

a) Jacob had to accept Leah first before Rachel could manifest.

b) You must accept the wife of your waking moment as the Raw material that will produce the wife of your dream.

c) Marriages fail and Singles are never able to marry because they are simply chasing dreams and ignoring reality.

d) You need to accept your wife of the waking moments first; and many Singles may need to accept that brother or sister for who they are rather always seeking illusory perfection.

3. **GOD ONLY USES THE WIFE OF YOUR WAKING MOMENTS TO BIRTH DESTINY & PURPOSE; NOT THE WIFE OF YOUR DREAM.**

a) There is a way that seems right to a man…the end of which is destruction.[40]

b) Jacob's wife of His waking moments (LEAH) birthed: Reuben, Simeon, Levi, Judah, Issachar, Zebulun, and Dinah)

    a. JESUS the Messiah came out of the tribe of JUDAH; birthed by the wife of his waking moment.

    b. The wife of your dream may not be consistent with God's plan for you, because your dream can evolve with time and you don't want a wife that is already

[40] Prov. 14:12

rigidly fixed to your previous dream.

4. GOD WILL ALWAYS ONLY GIVE YOU THE RAW MATERIALS AND NOT THE FINISHED PRODUCT.

a) The wife of your waking moment is the Raw material that will produce the wife of your dream.

b) You must begin with the wife of your waking moments, not the other way round. You must accept your spouse in reality before you can begin to mould each other into your dream spouses.

c) Your current spouse is the raw material with which to create your future in marriage.

5. **THE TRANSFORMATION OF YOUR WIFE (HUSBAND) IN REALITY TO THE WIFE OF YOUR DREAM ONLY TRULY BEGIN AS**

YOU MATURE AND YOUR DREAM IS GOD-LED.

a) Yes, have dreams and aspirations; but do not put God in a box and close the lid. God is always on the move.

b) You also need to know that God only reveals his plans to you only to the extent you can handle. He reveals more as you mature and obey Him. So Visions and aspirations should be flexible to reflect God's leadings.

c) God will give you a view of the THRUST of His purpose for you as you obey him; but the detail of every dream and actions to get there may be varied by Him from time to time.

"Then, being divinely warned in a dream that they should not return to Herod, they departed for their own country another way."[41]

[41] Matthew 2:12 (NKJV)

d) So God can lead you another way from the original plan....But the essence of the assignment will be the same.

e) If God is sending you to the south pole, marry for the assignment not just the path. (i.e. As a SINGLE, marry a spouse that can live in south pole...but don't marry one that can only travel by air. The path could change).

f) Give room the Changes you will both go through in marriage. You are both still work in progress.

6. **AS YOUR REAL SELF BEGIN TO TRANSFORM INTO YOUR DREAM SELF; THEN THE WIFE OF YOUR DREAM WILL ALSO BEGIN TO EMERGE. THUS THE TWO BEGINS TO BECOME ONE.**

a) The only dream that last is the dream that is fulfilled in reality. So making them ONE is the only way you can have a fulfilling marriage.

b) It has to be like for like. The wife of your dream cannot emerge to confront the real you (You of the waking moments). So you need to become the dream you before the wife of your dream can also emerge.

c) As you grow your spouse will grow

d) As you mature your spouse will mature.

e) As you transform to a DREAM you; then your wife will also be able to transform to a dream wife. You are in this together.

7. MAKING THEM ONE WILL REQUIRE HARD WORK.

a) Jacob laboured for 14yrs to be able to marry Rachel and then laboured for several more years after.

b) You will need to work hard and be persistent to make them one.

c) You must put more of your energy on changing yourself (and not your spouse)…because as you change, they will have little choice but to change as well.

    a. (e.g If you say your wife does not smile…you learn to begin to smile all the time you see her…sooner or later she will have no choice but to begin to smile back).

    b. So you change your spouse by changing yourself first. That is the only way.

God bless you as you use wisdom to make them one.

CHAPTER 5

UNDERSTANDING THE SEVEN Ms OF MARRIAGE

From this Chapter, I want us to examine the manufacturer's manual and mission for marriage. The challenge with marriage is many have allowed the world to define what it is and what it should look like. So if I ask you "What is a good marriage?"

I can assume your views would have been shaped (whatever answer you give) by Hollywood, Nollywood, Bollywood, parents, romance novels, friends, arts and entertainment in general.

But the question is what is a good marriage from a Biblical perspectives? From Genesis to Revelation, there is nowhere in the Bible, where Bible provides a complete and exhaustive list of what a good marriage consists of. This is because despite some commonalities that exists in marriages, each one is still unique.

Yes, it instructs husbands to love their wives and for wives to submit to their own husband.[42] We will discuss this scriptural instruction later in the Chapter.

Submission is in levels and what love is the Bible talking about here? There is more to these instructions than a casual glance will reveal. But there is nothing that says OK, these are the five things that if it is present then it is a good marriage. Why? Because marriage is about the two individuals involved.

What makes one couple happy, another couple would have exactly the same thing and they will not be happy. So how do you define a good marriage? You need to define your

[42] Ephesians 5:25 (NKJV)

own shape in God, rather than allowing somebody else to define it for you.

Many are at a place in their marriage, where others are envious of them and are saying, "I wish my marriage is like that". Yet they are complaining of their marriage that others envy. Ironic is it not?

Marriage was God's idea and invention. God said that it was not good for man to be alone…I will make an helper suitable for him God said.[43] So it was God that saw the need and designed a solution by creating the institution of marriage. Hence, it is essential that you understand the intention and purpose of the inventor to fully grasp how to make a success of the invention. Therefore in the following Chapters, we will be looking at what I call the seven Ms of marriage". These Ms will allow you to develop a 360 degree view of marriage as God intended.

---

[43] Genesis 2:18 (NIV)

So the idea of going through the seven M's of marriage is that by the time you understand all of them, your concept of marriage will change; because you will fully realise that many of the things and people you predicate your happiness on, are incapable of meeting your needs.

Knowledge of these seven Ms of marriage will help see you through the various turbulences and challenges that comes with marriage. You will be better equipped to deal with all challenges in marriage if you develop full understanding of these seven Ms. You will for instance be able to understand that marriage is not just about your happiness. There are single unhappy people, as well as single happy people. Hence marriage cannot guarantee happiness for you.

Marriage does not create happiness, people do. So ending your marriage because you are unhappy is not only foolish but can condemn you to a lifetime of unhappiness. Why? Because happiness depends on you and your reaction to what life and others throw at you. The same thing that makes you unhappy, makes the other fellow happy and makes the folk down the road indifferent. The situation is the same, it is the reaction and attitude of each individuals that is different. And that is what matters.

Many put on their spouse what only God can do, and an inevitable disappointment will follow. The greatest work in marriage is on yourself and not on your partner. The wise realises that as you change and transform yourself, you will change the response of your spouse as a consequence. The quickest way to change your spouse is to change yourself.

As you become better, you will force a positive response from your spouse. We all response to the change we see in others. If I see you and I am beaming with a big smile, you will have no choice but to respond by smiling too.

So by smiling, I am compelling a set response from you. So rather than make changing your partner your life's mission, focus on changing yourself. Improve yourself. Transform yourself. It is all about YOU. So what are the seven Ms of marriage we will be be exploring in the remaining chapters of this book?

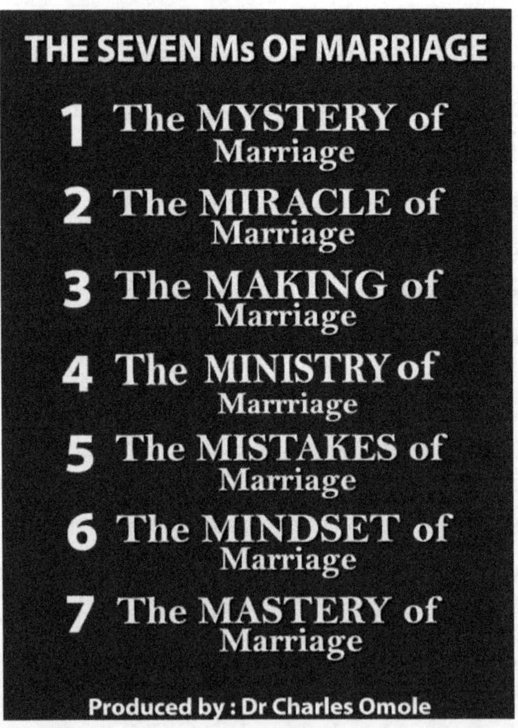

THE SEVEN Ms OF MARRIAGE
1 The MYSTERY of Marriage
2 The MIRACLE of Marriage
3 The MAKING of Marriage
4 The MINISTRY of Marrriage
5 The MISTAKES of Marriage
6 The MINDSET of Marriage
7 The MASTERY of Marriage
Produced by : Dr Charles Omole

Figure 5

CHAPTER 6

#1: THE MYSTERY OF MARRIAGE

The MYSTERY of Marriage

"For this reason a man shall leave his father and mother and be joined to his wife, and the two shall become one flesh. "This is ***a great mystery****, but I speak concerning Christ and the church.*[44]

The first **M** of marriage is the **"Mystery of Marriage"**. Marriage is a mystery. God said it is not good for man to be alone[45]. That statement confused me for a long time, because the Bible makes it clear that God came in the cool of the day to fellowship with Adam

[44] Ephesians 5:31-32
[45] Genesis 2:18

in the Garden. So how can man be alone if he is with God?

We commonly say that one with God is a majority, yet this guy was with God and God said that he was alone. There is a mystery in marriage that many do not understand.

Marriage is a spiritual institution and a great Mystery and like everything else that is a mystery, it will take more than a casual glance to fully understand it? Every mystery has a solution. It is just not commonly available.

If something is a mystery, it doesn't mean that there is nobody that knows the answer. It simply means that the answer requires you to dig deeper. So marriage is a mystery and its depth requires a life long commitment to learning. As a married person, you are part of a mystery set up by God, so you need to have the humility to accept the limitation of your understanding of this mystery and give yourself to learning about it and studying the word of God about it, instead of looking at how you can get out of the relationship.

This is why you can be married for forty years and you are still discovering new things about each other. You never fully know each other as you are continually learning, continually growing. That is the mystery of marriage.

Marriage is not a destination, it's a journey. So the question I want to ask you is this: How can you say your marriage is not good, when you know next to nothing about the mystery of the institution of marriage?

How can you conclude something is bad, when you know little about its full essence and basis for its existence? There are so many things about marriage that do not make sense in an increasingly selfish world.

How can you commit to one person for the rest of your life? This is a mystery. Only those that understand that marriage is not just a legal construct but a spiritual creation of God can truly begin to explore what is possible in marriage.

After writing more than half of the New Testament, right at the end of his ministry (after all the great encounters he had with the Lord), Apostle Paul was ending his ministry but with a profound statement. He said *"that I may know him; and the power of His resurrection"*; and I am astonished by Paul's statement. *If you don't know him, then the rest of us are in trouble…* I thought to myself.

This is very instructive. It appears that the more of God you know, the more you know you don't know God. God is indeed limitless.

So how can you conclude after 5 years of marriage that it is over, regardless of the challenges you are facing. You took an oath that stated *"…For better for worse...in sickness and in health…"* The trouble is 'who tells us what the worse is'? Who defines worse? You or God? What is worse for you may be just ok for somebody else in another relationship. The mystery of marriage is also revealed in its self-healing characteristics. Today you "hate" each other due to a disagreement but by the end of the week you are back in love again. This is a built-in sustaining feature of marriages by God.

Because you are constantly learning, you will realise that no matter how long you have been married, you are still learning new things about each other. Marriage is a mystery and you need to understand that first of all, because if you don't grasp the mysterious root of marriage, you would begin to think that it is all about the paper certificate that is given at the marriage registry.

That is why I am really not bothered by the wave of Gay Marriage legislations sweeping many countries. The State can legalize anything they like. It makes no difference; because the root of marriage is not in the paper certificate. Hence if the paper certificate is not the root of Christian marriage from God's perspective, then the paper certificate cannot define it adequately. It's like someone obtaining a paper certificate ordaining him as a Pastor. That means nothing if God did not call him into that office in the first place. The certificate means nothing to God. And God's enablement to function will be absent.

So it's very important, that you understand that you entered a mysterious institution and a divine covenant. God said it's not good for man to be alone. It is instructive that when God stated that it is not good for man to be alone, Adam was in God's presence and fellowshipped with Him daily. So how can man be alone when he is with God? That must mean God concluded that certain needs man has can only be met by somebody at his level. That even God cannot be a substitute for that. This is the beginning of that mystery.

The more you fellowship with God and learn about Him as a married person, the more you will realize that he will begin to reveal more and more to you. So the first M of marriage is the Mystery of Marriage.

CHAPTER 7

#2: THE **MIRACLE** OF MARRIAGE

The second **M** of Marriage is the **"Miracle of Marriage".** Besides salvation, marriage is one of the most miraculous thing that can happen to a Christian. It is a miracle. That's why the Bible says in the Book of Psalms 127 verse 1, unless the Lord builds a house, they labour in vain to build it.

There is a natural law called the *law of diminishing returns;* which means something can be exciting to start with but then natural law takes over and as you spend more time with that thing the excitement sort of diminishes over time. In economics; this is a law *affirming that to continue after a certain level of performance has been reached will result in a decline in effectiveness.*[46]

In sociological term this law is used to explain the diminishing excitement in a relationship as familiarity sets in over a period of time. For instance; if you have not seen someone for years, you get very excited when you see them again.

But after three months of daily contact, that excitement will recede as you get used to their presence.

This is what should naturally happen in a marriage. In a world that celebrate hedonism, overt sexual expression and plenty of alternative lifestyles; After seeing your spouse daily for ten years for instance, how can you still be emotionally excited by them? This is the Miracle of marriage.

---

[46] http://www.thefreedictionary.com/law+of+diminishing+returns accessed on 5 June 2016

How can a couple be married for forty years and then look at each other and are excited about each other as if it were day one. That is a miracle.

The miracle of marriage means that it does not follow the natural law of diminishing returns. It means you look at each other after years together and you're still excited. In fact your love gets better with years.

In Chapter Three, I explained the difference between pre and post marital love. Like previously stated, pre wedding love cannot sustain a marriage because it is not based on knowledge.

The miracle of the post wedding love is that you know more about the flaws of each other yet you love each other more. That doesn't make sense, that shouldn't make sense. It is a miracle.

So there is a miraculous element to marriage and that is why you must recognise that as a

Christian your marriage does not involve just the two of you. There is the third person in your relationship who is Christ.

You need to allow Christ to minister to you. This supports our discussion in earlier chapters that when you have a desire that is not met, give it to the third person present (Christ); and through the miracle of marriage, He will work things out for you; rather than you trying to work it out yourself and escalate it to demand.

Marriage is a miracle. It is not a natural union. It is a miraculous union. You must understand and accept this reality to have a fruitful, lasting and rewarding union.

CHAPTER 8

#3: THE **MINDSET** OF MARRIAGE

The third M of marriage is the "Mind-set" of Marriage.

One of the challenges many married people face, is the fact that they are married but are still thinking as if they are single. There is a mind-set needed to make marriage work and that paradigm shift needs to take place.

To fully understand this, you need to ask how and where did you form your belief system or paradigm of marriage?

It's absolutely important that you know that there is a new way of thinking that must be learned, to make marriage work.

PARADIGM SHIFT IN MARRIAGE

The Bible states that "*For as he thinketh in his heart, so is he*".[47]

When we are born, our understanding increases as we grow older to a point where we are able to make conscious judgements based on our will.

However, what is not known to many is that during this period of growing into adult consciousness; our Sub-conscious mind is being populated, trained and developed through repeated exposure to words, images, actions etc.

It is the content of our subconscious mind that creates our Paradigm and world view. Sub conscious mind is also called the unconscious mind. It is a mind you don't have an active relation with. It is partly genetic but mostly environmental

[47] Proverbs 23:7

The sub conscious mind is designed to keep us safe. It wants to use the memories of your past to keep you safe as it sees it. But it can be wrong.

It stores our value system based on our exposure from birth. As we learn new things consciously later in life, it is being filtered through the prism of the paradigm that has already developed in childhood. This determines ultimately what we do and what we attract into our lives.

Our conscious mind controls our Intellect, but it is in the unconscious mind that Paradigm resides. Paradigm is CULTURE, GROUP OF HABITS. So until we change our Paradigm or value system; any new things we learn will be of no value. Our paradigm determines what we hear from what we are hearing.

Every individual person has a unique belief system. There are similar systems of thought among various people but each and every human being has a very exclusive way of viewing the world around them.

Your individual belief system is made up of your thoughts and beliefs as well as the thoughts and beliefs that were handed to you at an early age before you were consciously able to choose what you think.

When your mind receives information it breaks it down into individual components, compares these bits of data to your existing beliefs and then takes this information and reassembles it as a mental construct.

The human mind basically interprets the data according to all of its past experiences. Two people can view the same "reality" and experience very different things since their experience is a result of the reconfigured mental construct and not the "reality" itself.

This mental construct is your personal version of the world that has been filtered through your current belief system and it creates a very specific signature vibration or frequency that is unlike any other person's.

So marriage is made of two people who have set paradigms of what a "good" marriage should look like. This mind-set or view of marriage was formed long before they met each other.

And in most cases these mind-sets are not based on the Word of God but on tradition, culture and paradigms developed from earlier in life.

But for a marriage to succeed, both partners MUST change their paradigms and consequently their mind-set about marriage.

So how do you change your Paradigm? Learning how to change your paradigm is so easy once you have a strong understanding of how one is created in the first place.

Paradigms or mind-sets, or what I call conditioning on a subconscious level are formed by constant repetition of ideas to someone on an emotional level. Once the idea is repeated enough it ultimately because fixed in the subconscious mind.

For instance, a boy that grew up in a family where the father believes that only women should cook and work in the kitchen will grow up with a mind-set or paradigm of the same value as his father. This will instantly shape his expectation of what his own wife should be doing at home. But this is a mind-set that is unscriptural yet holds many husband bound.

Everyone wants to change their paradigms but always miss the above concept completely. If you want better results in relationships as I'm sure most people do, you have to learn how to be able to access your subconscious mind where the paradigm is currently and begin to wash it by the washing of the water of the word.[48]

---

[48] Ephesians 5:26

Discarding paradigms that run contrary to the word of God. Because paradigms are embedded deep into our subconscious mind, many people actually belief in and trust their paradigms inspired world view than they believe the word of God.

So to Change your Paradigm, you must REPEATEDLY impress the word of God onto the conscious AND subconscious minds until it manifests through the change in your belief system, mind-set or paradigm.

Repetition is what "deprograms" your existing belief system and then "reprograms" it with the new desire and mind-set based on the word.

How long it takes to "reprogram" your belief system will depend upon two things:

- What you have believed in the past that is contrary to the new belief, and
- how often you impress the new directive onto the conscious AND subconscious minds.

Therefore, there is a mind-set needed to succeed in marriage; but many people do not come into marriage with that mind-set already in place.

So your duty as a married person is to begin to allow the word of God to cleanse and change your paradigm through your repeated study and confession of the word of God relating to marriage and relationship.

You cannot succeed in marriage holding on to your unscriptural culture based paradigms. You will be easily manipulated by the enemy to the detriment of your marriage.

For instance, one of the fundamentals I tell people is they must learn to believe the best of each other in marriage. It is natural paradigm to see, negative and the wrong thing in people.

Negative conclusion is a lot more instinctive to do than to have positive conclusion of the actions or motives of others.

So you and your spouse, have agreed about something. Now if he or she doesn't do what you have agreed, why don't you, believe that there must be a genuine reason, why that didn't happen as you agreed.

Rather than just jump to conclusion, *"She doesn't want to do it anyway"*, *"I knew she wouldn't do it"* and then when you hear the reason why he/she didn't do it, suddenly you find out that you are wrong. Why is it easier to jump to negative conclusions that positive? Because that is how many people have been trained based on their paradigms.

Why don't you prefer and choose the best option, in every situation. That's the mind-set needed to make marriage work; this is absolutely important. This mind-set inform your actions, it informs your conduct and more importantly, it actually reflects in your countenance. But you must actively learn this transformed mind-set by getting rid of your old paradigms.

There is a way you carry yourself, that people will know you are married. Listen folks, regardless of what you have in your finger or not have, if after ten years of marriage, you are mingling with colleagues and their friends and people can't tell that you are married; you need to look out. I am serious.

There is a way you carry yourself that people of the opposite sex will know without you even saying a word that this one is married.

But the point I am trying to make is that there's a mind-set needed in marriage.

This renewed mind-set is needed to help you deal with three key stress points in marriage.

Number One: ***Unexpected differences.*** Differences are not wrong they are just different.

Isn't it funny how before you got married you thinking to yourself, how similar you are and then the moment you got married you realize how different you are?

That's what shows you the dynamics have changed; but the point is, an unexpected difference is bound to happen in marriage. Think about it, how fun would it be to live with you? So you married somebody, who different; who thinks differently from you there's nothing wrong with that.

You know, there's a common statement in management parlance, which states that if a company has two members on their board and the two never disagree, one of them is unnecessary. Because why pay for two directors, who always thinking the same thing, might as well sack one and pay for one.

Clearly couple will inevitable have many similarities as well, but there must be differences too. And it is in these unexpected differences that conflict and problems starts in marriages.

Number Two: ***Unmet needs.***

This is one of the key areas wives need o bear with their husbands. Men sometimes can have very thick skinned and naïve. Sometimes men don't get it, you know. Sometimes things have to be right in front of our eyes before we see it.

So don't assume that men should be able to pick things from a mile away. We are not wired like that. There's a story of a couple that went to a counsellor as their marriage was in serious difficulty.

The counsellor counselled them for a few hours. So at the end the counsellor got up and gave the wife a parting kiss on the cheek; and the wife lit up, was happy; and the counsellor said to the husband *"you see this is what your wife needs every day,"* and the husband replied, *"I can only bring her twice a week."*

Now that shows you how sometimes men can be in their own world. The counsellor was saying one thing and he was thinking something else. The counsellor was talking about the need for the husband to show daily affection, but the man was thinking about bringing her daily to the counsellor. Typical man.

The point that I am making is that unmet needs is a major problem in relationships and we need to learn to cast all our cares on God. We discussed this problem of unmet needs in earlier chapters. But both parties must develop a renewed mind-set that is more tuned to each other's need.

And then the third thing that your new mind-set need to equip you for is:

Number Three: ***Unforgiven mistakes***

Your marriage is to an imperfect person; so there will be errors and shortcomings. There will be mistakes; and from our upbringing and from societal pressure, we are not adequately prepared to deal with the shortcomings of others. For example, we've learnt wrongly to classify sin and errors into small, medium and large, whereas with God sin is sin.

So a liar and murderer are equal in gravity to God. That is why God can forgive both sin; but in our upbringing these things have been given carnal human classifications of small, medium and big sins. Thus our response to sin is based on how small or big we think it is.

Hence your ability and ease to forgive your spouse depend on how small or big their mistake is. This is not a scriptural disposition at all.

Sin is sin; and if we understand that concept then it is easier to forgive each other. Unforgiven mistakes are a major problem that we need to deal with in marriages.

Developing the right mind-set for marriage is essential to a successful relationship. This is where I think the biggest problem lies, because our mind-set informs our expectations of our role and that of our spouse in marriage. And if these are based on our old paradigm rather than renewed mind-set; there will be trouble.

You have to prayerfully develop the right mind-set in marriage as you allow the word of God to renew and transform your mind.

For those newly married, this may take some time but you have to work at it. For long you are used to getting up and going whenever you want to travel; but now you need to discuss the trip with your spouse and make sure they are happy about it.

Things must change now that you are married. Your mind-set must be reset from single mode to married mode. Now it is no longer just about you alone. To succeed in marriage you need the right mind-set that is being renewed daily by the word of God, overwriting all paradigms and concepts.

For instance, I have seen many situations of ladies who grow up in homes where there are cooks and other servants in the house who cooked and did everything for them. They come into the marriage with that worldview that they as wives are not supposed to cook, wash or even tidy the home.

Conflict starts almost immediately. They have not reset their mind-set to married mode. Even if you can afford a cook, your husband may want to eat only your own cooked food. What do you do? Your mind-set must change.

You cannot succeed in marriage with all your old paradigms intact. You have to allow God to work on you and you must embrace the new you as a married man or woman.

Both parties in a marriage need to develop a new mind-set that will allow the marriage to flourish.

CHAPTER 9

#4: THE **MAKING** OF MARRIAGE

The forth **M** of marriage is the **"Making of marriage"**.

If you are making something, you must have an end state in mind. You must be shooting for an end game. So if your picture of that end game is wrong (unscriptural); then you are making and building a tower that will soon fall apart.

Sadly in too many cases, we pattern our marriages along something God did not design in the first place. As a result, we run into all kinds of difficulty. The first thing you need to understand about the making of your marriage is that it is primarily about the two of you. What works for somebody else may not work for you. The first rule of the Making of marriage is that each marriage is unique. This is because the parties involved are unique human beings, with unique paradigms, expectations, worldview and value systems.

You need to find what works for both of you. Remember there is no "the marriage"; there is "a marriage"; and "a" is yours. So you need to find what works for you; not try to plagiarise another marriage. You can learn things from others, but ultimately it is about the two of you; and there are certain ingredients **needed to make a marriage work.** Let us look at a few of them quickly.

Number 1: **Agape Love**; and I deliberately stressed the word Agape.

Emotional love cannot keep a marriage together. If you ask everyone that have gone through divorce, they will tell you that they loved each other at the beginning. So what happened to that love? It meant something happened that the love they had couldn't withstand. But that cannot be unconditional love (which is Agape). Because Agape love bears all things.[49]

Emotional love cannot sustain a marriage; you need agape love; the only unconditional love that exists is agape; the only love that can look at your faults and still say I love you is agape, not emotional. We already discussed this in previous chapters. We examined how romantic love (Eros) is largely a chemical reaction; it's not just you. There's a physiological dimension to that.

Love, the bible says does not insist on its own.[50] I have met couples where either the husband or the wife, if they are right about an issue, they are so bent on proving that rightness and don't care what damaged they cause along the way. As long as their rightness is accepted by the partner.

---

[49] 1 Corinthians 13:7
[50] 1 Corinthians 13:5

I ask myself why can't you just say you are wrong (at the moment in time) if that gives you peace. Your being right will be evident in the long run. So it's important that you understand that love prefers orders. You do whatever diffuses a tense situation.

Number 2: The second ingredient is **Loyalty**. The loyalty of husband to wife (and vice versa) is so sacrosanct that even the earthly legal system recognises it. That is why spouses cannot be compelled to give evidence against each other in court; because the evidence could be instantly tainted.

In fact what is discussed in the marital bed is considered private that it is only in very narrow circumstances that your spouse could be allowed to reveal it in court.

So loyalty is absolutely the key, you know, in marriage; and there are some sensitivities around loyalty that we need to understand. For instance, I tell spouses usually young ones, to avoid public disagreements with each other.

Especially the young ones who tend to be passionate about different topics and issues. I say, if you are outside and your husband takes a position about a topic, even if you don't agree with it, it may be wise to not oppose him publicly. It's may need you to either keep quiet or support him.

When you get home, you can actually say *"That's not my position"*, and discuss and debate the matter to your hearts content. Wisdom is profitable. Your marriage is not worth winning that one argument about. So it's absolutely important that you know loyalty is an essential ingredient in the making of a lasting marriage.

Number 3: The third ingredient is **Respect**.
Mutual respect is fundamental for any marriage that expects long term success. However, respect means different things to different people. For instance what is considered respectful can be culturally informed.

This disparity can be aptly explained by the fact that the man and woman in the marriage can say the same thing for instance. But that does not mean they meant the same thing. You see if a man tells the wife, "I don't trust you" and the woman tells the husband, "I don't trust you", they are not saying the same thing. They've said exactly the same words but research has shown that they're not saying the same thing.

In 95% of the occasion, when the wife says to the husband, I don't trust you, it involves fidelity; whereas if the husband tells the wife, I don't trust you in 95% of the situation it has nothing to do with fidelity or sexual transgression. Even though they use the same words but it is different things they are saying.

Men speak in straight lines; while women speak in circles. Hence, part of the skill a man need to develop is not only to look at what she's saying, look at what she is not saying and why she saying what she is saying.

So both parties have to communicate and understand what the other consider disrespectful. A lot of this may have to do with your culture and upbringing. But you must work to value what your spouse considers respectful and act accordingly.

You will find it difficult to attract into your life what/who you do not respect. To make a lasting marriage, you must respect each other and understand what each other value.

Number 4: The forth ingredient in the Making of a marriage is **Faithfulness**.

Couples in a marriage need to keep each other's confidence. Nobody should know more about you than your spouse. Keeping each other's confidence is an expression of faithfulness and commitment to each other. So, both parties have to avoid things that can lead to breakdown in this area.

For instance, you don't use against your husband in a future conversation, what he confided in you previously. He's not going to tell you his deep feelings again if you make that a habit. So you've got to help each other build that faithfulness. You've got to assist each other to build that faithfulness.

Understand that your spouse is not attempting to put you on a leash. It's simply a matter of honouring your commitment, and of letting your spouse know when to start worrying for instance. If you didn't want to be cared about or be responsible to someone else, you shouldn't have married. And you should not if still single. In marriage you are no longer just your own.

True commitment and faithfulness means to be trusted in all areas, not just the sexual department concerning matters of fidelity. Being faithful means that you are trusted with the matters of each other's hearts. Being faithful means that you can be depended upon to follow through with your promises.

It means that your partner should have a confident expectation (or faith in you) that you will follow through and deliver on not only your promises but your wedding vows as well. This kind of confidence helps to eliminate fear or worry in a relationship.

Number 5: The fifth ingredient is **Intimacy.** By intimacy I am referring to physical, spiritual and emotional intimacy.

Marriage should be the most intimate relationship anybody experiences in life. It should be more intimate than a friendship, a mother-daughter relationship, a father-son relationship, a boyfriend-girlfriend relationship, etc. But sadly, many couples often feel distant and alone in marriage.

Because man is body, soul, and spirit,[51] married couples must cultivate each aspect of their being in order to develop intimacy. They must cultivate their friendship (soul), their

---

[51] 1 Thess 5:23 and Heb. 4:12

sexuality (body), and their spirituality (spirit) in marriage. If one aspect of this tri-unity is missing, couples will lack the intimacy God desires. Therefore, all three must be continually cultivated.[52]

Intimacy also has to do with communication between couples. Women for instance just love talking. A woman is happy that just listened to her even if you proffered no solution to her problems. Men do not function that way. So a man will only talk to you, if he feels you have a solution to a problem. A man will not just talk to you for the sake of talking.

Talking is therapy for women and men need to develop the patience to accommodate the needs of their wives. This helps with emotional intimacy. So you just have to learn to listen.

In my research I found a material that can be of help to many husbands. It is titled *"30 ways*

---

[52] <https://bible.org/seriespage/8-foundation-eight-intimacy-marriage>

to be intimate with your wife".[53] So I have included it below with source reference in footnote. At least you cannot claim you lack ideas from now on.

Here are 30 ways to be intimate with your wife. Start today and by this time next month you'll be making the neighbours jealous.

<u>30 ways to be intimate with your wife.</u>

#1: Have a Picnic: Whether you have a picnic at the park, beach, or living room floor, sharing a blanket full of food is a simple yet terrific way to enhance intimacy. You could be sitting beneath a cloud-filled sky dreaming of what will one day be, or in front of the fireplace revelling in silence – the one-one-one without the usual distractions will reinforce the idea that all you need is each other.

#2: Take her to the ballet: Maybe your wife isn't the theatre type. But if ballet, opera or

[53] http://simplemarriage.net/30-ways-to-be-intimate-with-your-wife/

anything on the stage is something she would enjoy, two tickets for an evening at the theatre will show how much you care. Ballet or opera probably aren't for, but it isn't about you. Buying tickets shows an active interest in her.

#3: Book a room at a local bed and breakfast: This is a low maintenance way to experience the benefits of time away without emptying your bank account. Lavish your lover with a romantic evening and a leisurely breakfast, and let someone else do all the heavy lifting.

#4: Send flowers to work: Take it from me, a guy who worked in a flower shop for 12 years. Women LOVE getting flowers, especially at work. Having flowers delivered to your wife's workplace will make the women around her jealous. Imagine what that might do for you.

#5: Surprise her: Leave an hour early from work and have a nice dinner prepared when she gets home. Schedule a babysitter for the kids if you need to, but make the evening about the two of you.

#6: Prepare a gift basket full of romantic items: Your wife works hard. Sometimes all she wants is a break. Give her what she needs with a basket brimming full of bath salts, chocolates, bubble bath and scented candles. The basket does the hard work for you, providing her with a calm, relaxing (and accessible) escape from reality.

#7: Make a romantic memory scavenger hunt: I'm sure you remember back when you first started dating and intimacy wasn't a problem. Create a scavenger hunt built around your personal histories; your first kiss, first I love you!, or any old moment worth reliving. She'll love the memories!

#8: Give her public praise: Just as sending flowers to her workplace will build her self esteem and help her see you in a softer light, even when you're not around, praising her in public, whether she's present or not, will do the same - especially when she hears others repeating your words back to her.

#9: Make her breakfast in bed: It's cliché, but you can never go wrong with breakfast in bed (as long as you don't burn anything or settle for cold cereal!).

#10: Do your chores (and hers): Surprise her by completing a stray chore or lingering home project that's been laying unfinished for too long. Chipping in shows her you don't take her for granted. Whether you're helping to potty train your toddler, or finally finishing building the deck, your extra set of hands won't go unnoticed.

#11: Maintain eye contact: Great eye contact sends the signal that your partner's words are important to you. It shows your interest and affection. This will make your wife feel valued.

#12: Talk about your goals, then record them together: Discuss what you want for your collective future, then write those goals and set a date to re-evaluate them every six months. This will this make a great date night, but more importantly, it will establish a tradition of bonding that will keep you growing as a couple.

#13: Give her a seven second kiss: No need to hurry. Give her the same lingering lips you once did, back before she did all your laundry and you mailed all the bills.

#14: Be a better listener: Intimacy is about understanding and appreciating your wife's desires and interests. Being a better listener means more than not watching TV while she's talking, it's about caring enough to ask the questions that will fertilize the conversation.

#15: Have a mini-honeymoon: Make time to get away for a long weekend. How long has it been since the two of you spent significant time alone together? Chances are, you're overdue. Choose a special spot to get away from it all, and use your time to learn a little more about each other.

#16: Have manners: Be a gentleman. This may not seem like a big deal, but courtesy might be a bigger turn on for your Mrs. than you realize. Don't let chivalry die on your watch; open the door, pull out her chair and by all means, use the manners your mama gave you.

#17: Let her rest: When the kids rise in the middle of the night, or are up first thing Sunday morning, take the initiative to lead the family toward quiet. Bonus points if you take her out to breakfast when she wakes up!

#18: Put her goals first: If your wife wants to go back to school, make sure she has the chance. Whether she wants to learn sewing or scuba diving, give her time to learn and grow herself. If your wife feels like she's growing as a woman and person, she will be happier and healthier – so will your entire family.

#19: Write a mission statement: Take the time to write the expectations for your marriage and family. Sitting down and sharing goals is an extremely intimate experience. Deciding where to take your family together is the first step in getting where you've always wanted to go.

#20: Renew your wedding vows: You can't do this one often, but it's guaranteed to carry a lot of capital when you do!

#21: Ask your wife about her fears: Find out what makes her most insecure. This might even be uncomfortable, but only for a bit, and true intimacy is sometimes built by asking tough questions. Schedule a romantic dinner. Then ask what makes her sad and listen to her every word. Offer suggestions when appropriate, but it's most important to simply listen.

#22: Alleviate her fears: Find ways to alleviate her fears and insecurities. Use your new knowledge to help your wife find a better outlook. Let her know you are there to put her first and protect her forever.

#23: Put her first: Value your wife above everyone else and make sure she knows how you feel. Your friends will always be around, your parents are family, but your wife should feel like she's the most important person in your orbit.

#24: Court her: Remember how easy intimacy seemed before you said, "I do!" Intimacy doesn't end after you get married, but it's up to you to bring it back. You've caught her, but that doesn't mean she doesn't ever want to be chased.

#25: Spend quality time together: Invite her for some quality alone time. Mark it on the calendar and don't let anything get in the way. She deserves the attention and will appreciate having it.

#26: Write love letters: Making your feelings permanent with ink will go a long, long way. You don't have to be Shakespeare to express your affection. Write from your heart. She will love it.

#27: Show her intimacy without expectation: Show her how much you love her without wanting anything in return. She will likely give you things you weren't even asking for.

#28: Make her feel noticed: Let her know she looks beautiful when she takes the time to look pretty. Humans crave attention, you're wife's no different. Pay attention when she goes the extra mile and compliment her as often as possible.

#29: Recreate your first date: Tell your wife you're taking her out, but don't tell her where you're going. You may be inhibited by time or geography, but do your best to recreate the experience of your first date together.

#30: Take dancing lessons: Not only is this fun and intimate, taking dancing lessons together will ultimately lead to the two of you going out and practicing what you learned – then returning home electrified.

Intimacy is more than a physical desire; it's learning who your lover is on a deeper, more emotional level; discovering her interests and affections, and learning to appreciate the same things, at least on some level.

Take a month or two, try some of these ideas. Then keep it up.

So these are the key ingredients in the making of a marriage. This shows that the making of a good marriage requires your input and active innovation and sensitivity.

Your marriage cannot be made without your input. You set the tone and the pace for it. You have the divine resources already given to you. So step out in faith and begin to enjoy your marriage as God intended.

CHAPTER 10

#5: THE **MINISTRY** OF MARRIAGE

The fifth M of Marriage is what I called "The Ministry of Marriage".

By the Ministry of Marriage I'm not talking of marriage ministry in the Church as in, evangelism ministry or music ministry. That's not what I am referring to. I am discussing the Ministry dimension of the purpose for marriage.

How did the word Christian come? The word Christian came out of when they saw the way they were behaving, they said, "This men are behaving just like Christ". So as a result the word Christian was evolved to show those who behave like Christ. The Bible says, "The kingdoms of this world will become the kingdoms of our God.

God's purpose on the earth, is to raise a specimen of people that others will see and say, "Wow, I want what they've got". When it comes to marriage, God's core unit to exemplify his life on the face of the earth is the family unit. So you have to understand therefore, that Christian marriage is not just about you two; there is a ministry wide dimension of marriage.

In other words, there is a purpose God wants to achieve through your marriage, that has nothing to do with the two of you; that has to do with Him and His purpose.

So you need to understand that your happiness or your lack of it should not really become a factor. "Pastor I'm not happy". "So what?"

How many of you are happy going to work? Think about it. You're going to work but you're not happy and you still go to work. Why? Because it is your duty. And it pays the bill.

Exactly; there are so many things you do every day that you're unhappy doing and you still do it; because it is a necessity. So what gives you the impression you have to be happy all the time in marriage? Your happiness or sadness is not a factor caused my marriage alone. There are sad and miserable single people. So being single does not guarantee happiness either.

It's not about your happiness anymore. For instance, you have to buy petrol for your car. Right? Do you love petrol? No. Do you drink it? No. You still have to buy it; and whatever the price you pay. Why? Because you car needs it to perform. You don't buy it because you are happy.

So there are some things that are necessary, regardless of how you feel. People have reduced marriage to, "I don't feel happy so I quite."

Now, I'm not belittling the issue of happiness. If clearly for the entirety of your marriage you're unhappy throughout that's a problem that need addressing and that is a different matter altogether. But there will be phases and periods when you are unhappy. But you must get on with it. That doesn't mean it will always be like that.

You must know that there is a Ministry dimension to marriage that has nothing to do with you or your spouse but all to do with God's purpose for the institution.

Why is it that every time God wants to do something, he looks for a witness. He says, *"There's something I want to do in the city and I looked around to see if I could find just one man and I found none".* Why? Because God understand that based on His principle set up on the earth; if you are to function legitimately on the face to the earth, you have to be somebody born of a woman. So whenever God want to do something in a city, he looks for a man. Man here doesn't mean gender but mankind. God looks for a man that can model His presence.

There is a ministry dimension to marriage, that overrides your personal agenda. God wants to show you off to the world. He is counting on your obedience and projection of His purpose.

The ministry of marriage means you don't abandon a marriage simply because you think you don't love each other any more. There is a purpose for that relationship that is beyond you. And love (Eros) is linked to your feelings, therefore subject to change. Love can easily be rekindled if you remain in the place where grace can locate you.

It's like a pastor who wakes up on Sunday morning with bad head ache and pains in his hands and all over the body. And left to him, he will stay at home but he quickly realise that people are waiting for him in church, so he heads to church regardless of his pains. He probably will still be smiling as he lay hands on people during service; even when those hands are giving him pains. Why will the pastor do this? Because it is his calling and duty to be the pastor of that church. So he performs his duties regardless of his personal pain and challenges. This is same with the ministry of marriage. You stay and keep cultivating your marriage regardless of your personal feelings.

Remember, we have already discussed in previous chapters how the love needed to sustain marriage is first Agape love before Eros (Romantic love). The unconditional nature of Agape is needed to keep you married while working on fixing your challenges. If God admonishes us to love (agape) our enemies (that do nothing for us); how much more our spouses.

God knew that someone born of a woman is needed to give effect to what he wants to do on the earth. God has family in heaven but also on the earth; and He wants others to look at His family on earth be desirous of what they have, so much so that they give their life to Him also. So when you get married that's what you're making, you're saying, *"I am now a family unit that represents God"*. I model God's best and purpose in my marriage. Hence why I said it is not just all about you.

So whether you are happy or unhappy, it makes no difference. You just have to grow up and stop being led by changing feelings and emotions. You know why it makes no difference? Because what makes you happy or not happy is a function of your knowledge and maturity. It is not the act in itself.

There are certain things that were happening in the first year in your marriage that made you unhappy, if the same thing were to happen now you would just brush over it isn't it? What changed? You now know better and you are more matured. So the action has not changed, but its impact on you has changed. It no longer affect you like it used to. What if you have ended your marriage due to unhappiness in year one? You would have made a big mistake.

The action is the same, but the effect on you is different. So why must you end your marriage in year one because you are unhappy? You can see that the problem was not the action; it was the lack of maturity and knowledge to deal with that situation.

So that's what I mean by happiness is transient. It's purely your perception of what you are seeing; and your perception of what you are seeing is a function of your knowledge and maturity in God. You can't therefore say that you want to end things because you're unhappy today; because the same thing will happen next year and you're now grown in God and suddenly it makes no difference to you anymore.

So that's what I mean by happiness is overrated. I'm not trying to belittle your unhappiness. I'm merely saying your happiness or lack of it is based on your response to what you see around you and your knowledge to handle what you see around you increases all the time. It's not a function of what is happening, it's a function of your maturity to deal with it.

I read a book years ago (cannot remember the title) that said that the quantification of what Abraham rejected (gold, silver and so on) from the battle of the Kings is worth Billions of dollars today. Now what is it that Abraham our father has found?[54] The Bible said, he saw a city without foundation, whose builder and maker is God.[55]

For a man to reject Billion of dollars he must have seen (and found) something much bigger. Although with his spiritual eyes, it was nevertheless, very real to him. So your happiness or lack of it is not a product of what is happening around you; it's a product of

[54] Romans 4:1
[55] Hebrews 11:10

what you have found or seen and what you are seeing can inform what you reject or accept now. It can determine the level of your endurance.

So how can you want to end your marriage because of something happening currently, that is making you unhappy because of your perception of it now. When the same thing will happen in five years time, and you will not even be bothered by it. Many of you who have stayed with your marriage can now look back and see that what used to make you unhappy, now no longer bother you at all. You have matured. You have adapted. You are more knowledgeable.

So the ministry of marriage means you persist at it regardless of your unhappiness. Why? Because things will change eventually. It is your duty to keep your marriage. God is counting on showing you off to the world proudly. Learn to endure like a good soldier.

Looking at many of our parents, whose marriages have endured for decades. Is it because our fathers were saints? Not at all. They determined not to end the marriage no matter what happened. They endured. And many are reaping the rewards today.

As couples grow older, their excesses tend to diminish. A sense of legacy begins to set in that they become more interested in what the future hold for their children than their own lustful and behavioural shenanigans.

So don't make a crisis out of something transient. You should keep it in context, move on and that's the road to a solution. You must understand the Ministry of Marriage requires that you keep at it regardless of how you feel.

- **A strong marriage sanctifies the home.**

A marriage that is lived out according to the principles of the Word of God is a marriage that keeps God at the centre. It produces a home where Jesus is King and God is

Sovereign. It is a marriage that opens the door for God to bless in amazing ways. It is a marriage that invites the power of God to dwell in the home.

- **A strong marriage glorifies the saviour.**

A marriage that operates according to the principles of God's Word brings glory to the Lord. God is glorified when we live out our marriages according to His precepts. This is true because a marriage that functions according to the Word of God is a marriage that honours His will, and doing His will always brings glory to His name! So, God is glorified when we love like He does.

- **A strong marriage is a witness to the lost.**

A strong godly marriage is a witness to this lost generation because it is a living, breathing example of Christ and His church. It demonstrates the power of the love of God and the grace of God to all who witness it.

A godly marriage exemplifies forgiveness, patience, love, hope, and the power of God's saving grace. A GOOD, GODLY MARRIAGE

IS A POWERFUL WITNESS TO A LOST WORLD.

- **A strong marriage instructs the next generation.**

We need to realize that our children learn about marriage and about how to treat their future spouse by watching us.

When the world looks at our marriages, they should see how Christ loved His church. They should see that there is just something different about our love for our spouse. THIS IS THE MINISTRY OF MARRIAGE.

There are certain things, you don't do and you endure, not because it is wrong for you to do it, but because you know others will be messed up if you do it. You need to understand that.

That's what Apostle Paul meant when he said that, *"If any of those who do not believe invites you to dinner, and you desire to go, eat whatever is set before you, asking no question for conscience' sake.*

But if anyone says to you, "This was offered to idols," do not eat it for the sake of the one who told you, and for conscience' sake;[b] for "the earth is the Lord's, and all its fullness." "Conscience," I say, not your own, but that of the other. For why is my liberty judged by another man's conscience?[56]

He said, Don't eat it. Not because it is wrong in itself but because the weak in faith will be confused. They don't know what you know, so don't eat it. All things are lawful not all things are expedient.[57] So it is important therefore for you to understand you are an epistle others are reading and watching. You must maintain your ministry to strengthen their faith for their own ministry.

So there are certain things you curtail, not because it's wrong for you to do, but because you know are now an example to others. That's what marriage is all about. You're not happy in it, but stay in it, work on it. There is

---

[56] 1 Corinthians 10:26-29
[57] 1 Corinthians 10:23

nothing that is good and precious that comes that's not been worked on.

Champions are birth in the furnace of affliction, you need to go through process. Pruning. Brokenness. God never gives you the finished product. The more you complain about your spouse, the more you actually forget how flawed an individual you yourself are. Yet you are in judgment of others. This is the Ministry of Marriage. As a married person, you have been called and ordained into that ministry. Do not let God down.

Work at it. Pray at it. Learn at it. Grow at it. Throw everything at it. You will not drown, says the Lord. He will become the wind beneath your wings. Pay the price to make your calling and election sure. Change has come to your home today. It shall all end in praise in Jesus name.

CHAPTER 11

#6: THE **MISTAKES** OF MARRIAGE

The sixth M of marriage is the Mistakes of Marriage. The goal of this chapter is not to list all the mistakes people make in marriages. That will be an unending list. But I want to just quickly deal with the overarching mistakes that is common to all.

The biggest mistake that can take place in your marriage is your belief. That is; for you to believe that your marriage cannot change. That is the biggest mistake, because you are seeing the Pharaoh today and you think all is lost.

The key mistake of marriage is trying to conduct your marriage life based on the world's system; thinking that it cannot change. Everything in this life, including every marriage can change. But you must be willing to pay the price.

The bible says about God that He will not crush the weakest reed or put out a flickering candle.[58]

So if for instance there are fifty links that join you and your spouse together. The Bible is saying even if forty nine of them are broken; God will nature the only one remaining link and use that one link to heal the marriage. The biggest mistake in a marriage is either party believing it cannot be changed or rescued.

When we discussed the Mind-set of marriage earlier in the book, I explained how many people come into marriage with pre-determined ideas of what it should look like.

---

[58] Isaiah 42:3

But these ideas were informed by culture, customs, Hollywood, Nollywood, Bollywood and all the woods. There is now the challenge of renewing and transforming your paradigm through the word of God. A mind that is not transformed will lead to needless mistakes in marriage.

There's no fixed destination for everybody. What works for you, may not work for the next person. So you as a couple need to agree what that destination is, rather than comparing yourselves with somebody else.

I will like to repeat again that the key mistake of marriage is to try to conduct your marriage life based on the World's system and values. Only a Manufacturer can fully understand his product. Similarly, only God as the architect of marriage can fully understand how it can work and resolve any problem. Become fully reliant on God's methods only.

Many Christian marriages have collapsed simply because they chose to obey the rules of the world rather the word/rules of God. Invest your time in knowing and reading the manufacturer's manual, which is the word of God. Then build your marriage according to scriptural pattern. I will advise you read again the chapter on the Mind-set of marriage. This can help you prepare the right heart-ground to avoid the mistakes of marriage.

CHAPTER 12

#7: THE **MASTERY** OF MARRIAGE

The seventh M of marriage, is the Mastery of marriage which comes from appreciation of the mission of Marriage. The Mastery of Marriage is a journey not a destination.

Your mastery does not mean you know it all, but that you have reached a point where it is settled in your heart that your marriage is here to stay regardless of what you face. But more importantly, you are actively developing and growing your marriage day by day.

After submission and obedience to God, the only other tool needed to have Mastery of Marriage; is for you to understand how to deal with the challenges posed by the world's system against marriages.

The Bible says:

"*Therefore everyone who hears these words of mine and puts them into practice is like a wise man who **built his house** on the rock. The **rain** came down, the **streams** rose, and the **winds** blew and beat against that house; yet it did not fall, because it had its foundation on the rock. But everyone who hears these words of mine and does not put them into practice is like a foolish man who built his house on sand. The rain came down, the streams rose, and the winds blew and beat against that house, and it fell with a great crash.*"[59]

From this scripture we can see the three main challenges against marriages from the world system that we need to master.

- Rains are the culture you live in.

---

[59] Matthew 7:24-27 (NIV)

- ❖ Floods are the crises you live through in marriage.
- ❖ Winds are the changes you live with in marriage.

#1: The CULTURE you Live in.
Understand that our society is not the place to learn how marriage should be. It is full of ungodly unions & relationships. Make the WORD of God alone your standard.

So, what is the rain that beat against your marriage? The rain that beat against your marriage is the culture that you live in. You need to understand that the culture that you live in is the culture that does not help marriage.

It's not a culture that strengthens the institution of marriage. You can get marriage license in 5 minutes but it takes you weeks to get a car license.

The culture we live in is the more liberal, hedonistic culture is only about the individual.

Doing what makes a person happy is the golden rule.

This is the concept that is leading to all the changes that we see in our society; because it's whatever makes the individual happy is ok.

All kinds of nonsense are beginning to happen in the nations, all in the name of what makes the individual happy. That's not God's standard. God has the better standard. So if you understand that is the nature of the society you live in, you need to guard your marriage against it. Rather than embrace the culture, you need to understand that they are supposed to be looking at you and copying what you do. Not that you copy what they do and you become like one of them.

Remember the mountain of the Lord's house is exalted above all mountains.[60] So if marriage is a mountain, so the marriage of the Lord's house should be higher than all other

---

[60] Isaiah 2:2

mountains, that all the other marriages will look at it and say let us go into the house of the Lord. Because all the fruits of life dwell in Zion. So the rain is the culture you live in.

#2: The CRISIS you will live through.
This is the Flood. So the second thing that beat against the house is the flood. The flood is the crisis you're going to live through in marriage.

You need to understand that if you are married long enough, there are all kinds of crises that will set in that will test that marriage:

- bereavement,
- loss of job for a long time; and not having any job;
- financial difficulty;
- health issues;

The list is endless. You know there are so many crises that the marriage will live through that you need to be prepared for. You must understand how to deal with the crisis that you're going to go through even if that hasn't happened to you yet, it will happen. This is how you develop mastery of marriage.

If you are going on the journey and you've not met Satan then you're going in the same direction as he is. Because if you're going in opposite direction one day will be up clash, because crisis are inevitable.

Because the enemy hates you; so crisis are bound to happen. You got to learn to deal with all these crisis and the more you learn to deal with them the more you keep your marriage together.

#3: The CHANGES you are going to live with.

There will be PHYSICAL, EMOTIONAL & SPIRITUAL changes as you grow in marriage. You must be prepared for these. You have to love each other for WHO you are not What you have or Possess.

The wind represents the changes that you're going to live with. Folks everybody change;

spiritually, emotionally and particularly physically. Everybody change.

Changes are inevitable and that's why I say never fall in love with the physical body. Fall in love with a person, not a body part. Oh I love my wife's legs some will shout. I say to them, *"Eh, Eh. God help you if something happens to those legs. We will see what happens to your marriage."*

You see, it shouldn't be about about what we have, but who we are. Small, medium or large, your spouse still the same person. As you grow older, you may not be able to shift all the weight like you used to do. So enjoy your life and remain fit whatever your size. Change is inevitable in life and in marriage.

You've got to find ways of handling the changes that is inevitable in your marriage. You love your wife, because she was skinny; after one or two children suddenly she couldn't shift the baby weight gain anymore and then what happens? She's still your wife; she's still beautiful. I'm so content with this that I told my wife it doesn't matter what size you are; if you are thin, you are thin, if you are big, it makes absolutely no difference to me.

And that's the best place to be. The wind represents the changes that you're going to live through.

The Bible reassures us that:
"God says, `Don't be afraid. When you go through deep waters and great trouble, I will be with you. When you go through rivers of difficulty, you will not drown."[61]

So, you need to understand the MYSTERY of Marriage; the MIRACLE of Marriage, the MINDSET of Marriage, the MAKING of Marriage, the MINISTRY of Marriage, avoid the MISTAKES of Marriage and be ready to achieve a MASTERY of Marriage.

---

[61] Isaiah 43:1-3

Understanding these SEVEN Ms of Marriage will equip you for a blissful and rewarding marriage life.

The mastery of marriage is the end goal for all believers. This is when you enter God's rest in marriage. It requires knowledge and patience. It requires sensitivity to the voice of the Spirit of God to guide you. At this stage, you marriage becomes a poster of Christian marriage. You are not perfect, but your perfecting your marriage daily.

Wishing you God's blessings as you take on the charge. I am rooting for you. You will succeed. Blessings galore.

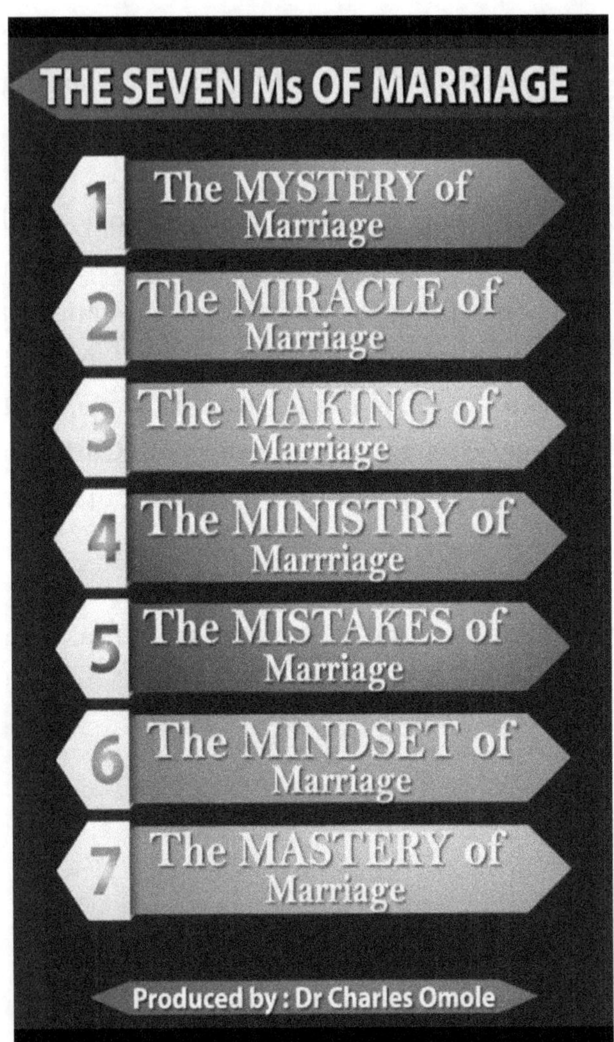
THE SEVEN Ms OF MARRIAGE
1 The MYSTERY of Marriage
2 The MIRACLE of Marriage
3 The MAKING of Marriage
4 The MINISTRY of Marrriage
5 The MISTAKES of Marriage
6 The MINDSET of Marriage
7 The MASTERY of Marriage
Produced by : Dr Charles Omole

Fig 6

BOOKS BY DR OMOLE

1) Church, Its time to Fly -- *Learning to fly on Eagles Wings*
2) How to Avoid Getting Hurt in Church -- *13 Steps that will protect you and help create an atmosphere for breakthroughs.*
3) Must I go to Church? 8 Reasons why you must attend Church.
4) Freedom from Condemnation -- *Breaking free from the burden and weight of sin.*
5) I cannot serve a big God and remain small
6) How to start your own business
7) How to Make Godly Decisions
8) How to Avoid Financial Collapse
9) Let Brotherly Love Continue: *An insight into love and companionship.*
10) Breaking Out of the Debt Trap
11) Common Causes of Unanswered Prayer.
12) How to Argue with God and Win -- *Biblical strategies on getting God's attention for all your circumstances all of the time*

13) Avoiding Power Failure-- *How to generate spiritual power for daily success and victorious living.*

14) How Long Should I Continue to Pray when I Don't See an Answer?

15) Success Killers: Seven Habits of Highly Ineffective Christians.

16) The Financial Resource Handbook - UK Edition

17) Divine Strategies for Uncommon Breakthroughs: Living in the Reality of the Supernatural

18) Keys to Divine Success

19) Wrong Thoughts, Wrong Emotions and Wrong Living

20) Secrets of Biblical Wealth Transfer

21) Journey to Fulfilment

22) Prosperity Unleashed - *A Definitive Guide to Biblical Economics*

23) No More Debt - Volume 1

24) Understanding Dominion

25) Advancement

26) Getting the Story Straight

27) Overcoming when Overwhelmed
28) The Spiritual Fitness Plan
29) Spiritual and Practical Steps to Commanding Value
30) Breakthrough Strategies for Christians in the Marketplace
31) Spiritual Keys to Financial Reward
32) Supporting Good Governance in Law Enforcement in African Societies
33) The 7Ms of Marriage

For more information about our ministry, world outreaches and a free catalogue of our media and study materials, please write to:

Winning Faith Outreach Ministries

151 Mackenzie Road

London. N7 8NF

UNITED KINGDOM

www.charlesomole.com

Email: **Info@Charlesomole.com**

www.ingramcontent.com/pod-product-compliance
Lightning Source LLC
LaVergne TN
LVHW051056080426
835508LV00019B/1902
9781907095160